"If you eat, you substitute. If you cook…well, we've all been there. The unexpected expired ingredient. The out-of-season ingredient. The 'thought I had enough of that spice, herb, or flavoring' ingredient…Becky Sue Epstein is a master of detail. She is respectful of tradition and environmentally sensitive remedies for the kitchen and home. The woman never tires of learning and sharing. *Substituting Ingredients* is a convenient tool and a good read, especially if you eat, drink, cook, or clean."

—Lynn Krielow Chamberlain, host, iWineRadio.com

"If there were ever an idea so practical and obvious that nobody else but Becky Sue Epstein could think of it, it's *Substituting Ingredients*."

—Charles Perry, *Los Angeles Times* food writer, retired

"So many of my cookbook readers email me with questions about substitutions. Now I have a resource for myself and for all of you who are inquisitive in the kitchen, willing to think outside the box, but still want good results. Becky Sue Epstein's *Substituting Ingredients* will be on my shelf with my treasured reference books; I am sure I will refer to it again and again."

—Dede Wilson, author of *Unforgettable Desserts*; dedewilson.blogspot.com

"With this paperback on the shelf there's no need for mad, mid-recipe dashes to the grocery store."

—*Bon Appétit*

Substituting Ingredients

The A to Z Kitchen Reference

BECKY SUE EPSTEIN

Published by Sourcebooks, Inc.
P.O. Box 4410, Naperville, Illinois 60567-4410
(630) 961-3900
Fax: (630) 961-2168
www.sourcebooks.com

Library of Congress Cataloging-in-Publication Data

Epstein, Becky Sue.
  Substituting ingredients : the A to Z kitchen reference / by Becky Sue Epstein. —
4th ed.
      p. cm.
  1. Cookery. 2. Ingredient substitutions (Cookery) I. Title.
  TX652.E58 2010
  641.5—dc22

                          2009049932

        Printed and bound in the United States of America.
                  VP 10 9 8 7 6 5 4

Thanks to Hilary Dole Klein, Lauren Garvey, Sheila Carme, Branko, and the rest of my family and friends who ate many strange things yet still encouraged me in the pursuit of my substitutions goals.

I am proud to carry on the traditions of my grandmother Gertrude, who was a caterer and cookbook writer, and my mother Doris, who loves to experiment with new recipes— but will make the old favorites when we need them.

Table of Contents

Introduction

Do any of these scenarios sound like something that has happened to you?

- Rushing into the kitchen, grabbing pots and pans and the ingredients for a favorite, last-minute dinner, you're dismayed to discover you're lacking a key ingredient.
- Perusing a magazine, you settle on an enticingly simple recipe, but then you notice it has a couple ingredients you're sure can't be found locally.
- Finally ready to try that friend's fabulous recipe you printed out some time ago, you suddenly realize you might not have all the ingredients—in fact, you're not exactly sure what one of them is...

What to do?

After this happened to me a few times, I started to accumulate substitutions for a variety of ingredients. The list grew until it became a collection. And then a project. For many months, my family and friends sampled a lot of strange foods. Finally, it turned into my first book, *Substituting Ingredients*.

I—and about a hundred thousand other people—used this collection of substitutions for more than fifteen years, through multiple printings and successive, updated editions.

Attitudes toward food, cooking, take-out, and eating out have continued to evolve. We're all much more adventuresome now, so it's time for a new edition.

This book is simple to consult and much more comprehensive than previous editions. It contains all the spices, herbs, exotic fruits, and vegetables needed for modern cooking, so you can actually prepare the exotic recipes you see online, in print, or on television every week.

It's great if you've just forgotten to buy a critical component for a recipe, something as basic as lemon juice or eggs. Perhaps you don't have time to search for a rare item, like fresh Alaskan King crabmeat, or you don't want to gamble on an expensive ingredient you might only use once, such as saffron.

Substituting Ingredients contains over 1,000 substitutions and easy directions to make dozens of common condiments. There are tables for converting, measuring, and determining temperature equivalents, as well as instructions for simple formulas for household cleaners.

Whether you're making an easy weekday meal or an elaborate dinner for a celebration, whether you have time constraints, financial restrictions, or food allergies, once you have this book in your kitchen, you'll use it again and again.

How to Use This Book

A TO Z INGREDIENTS

The largest section of this book is simply an A to Z reference. Look up an ingredient from your recipe, and you will find a substitution. If several substitutes are listed, the best match is the first one. It provides the closest match to the flavors of the original, taking into account the way the ingredient is most commonly used. When the substitutions are all very similar, the list is in alphabetical order. If there is no measure given for an ingredient, then the substitutes can generally be used in equivalent amounts.

For example, the listing for the herb chervil gives several substitutions. First is tarragon, with the instructions to use ½ the amount, which means that tarragon has the closest flavor but tends to be much stronger than chervil. Next is anise, with the same instructions, because it is a little less similar but also stronger than chervil. Next is Italian parsley, which is slightly different in flavor, but will also season a dish nicely.

If a recipe calls for a small amount of one type of fruit, another may be substituted, or the ingredient can be omitted. For example, ¼ to ½ cup raisins can be left out of a cookie or cake without affecting the chemistry of baking or cooking—though this will, of course, affect the flavor. The same is true of small amounts of meats or vegetables in savory dishes, usually up to ½ cup.

Remember: let your own preferences be your ultimate guide, and taste as you go.

Baking

Certain substitutions are standard in baking recipes. For instance, butter, margarine, blends, and even shortening can usually be used interchangeably without dramatically affecting the flavor or texture of the baked goods. Other baking substitutions can be more delicate processes, because it is important to keep the ratio of liquid ingredients to dry ingredients as close as possible to the original recipe.

Baking times may vary, so do be sure to monitor items and test for doneness.

Different types of sugar can be substituted for each other fairly easily. There is also a simple formula for composing baking chocolate from cocoa powder and butter.

Dairy Products

Substitutions are most critical when dairy products are cooked. It's generally not a good idea to heat yogurt or sour cream because they can separate. But for garnishes and dips, yogurt or sour cream can be often used in place of cream for a tangier taste or a lower fat content.

Otherwise, there are simple substitutes you can easily learn. For example, milk can be used in place of heavy cream or light cream in many recipes, with one or two essential additions.

Herbs, Spices, and Flavorings

Herb and spice substitutions depend on nuance, as well as personal preference. In this book, the first substitute in the list is generally closest to the original in flavor and/or texture, and takes into consideration the most common use of the spice or herb and whether it's for sweet or savory recipes. Sometimes combinations of ingredients are needed to achieve the flavor of the original. The substitution for fresh, grated ginger, for instance, is powdered ginger (about ¼ the amount originally called for) with a dash of white pepper and lemon juice. Or you can get candied or crystallized ginger and wash off the sugar before dicing it into your dish.

In general, 1 tablespoon of a fresh herb is the equivalent of 1 teaspoon of a dried herb.

When using dried herbs, crush them in the palm of your hand to release their flavors before mixing into the rest of the ingredients. After adding dried herbs and/or powdered spices, cook (or stir) for several minutes then taste before adjusting flavors further.

Wines, Spirits, and Flavorings

Wines and spirits are often used in cooking to add flavor. The alcohol evaporates quickly. For both red and white wines, use the drier rather than the sweeter styles. Specialty fortified wines such as marsala, sherry, and port intentionally add a little sweetness as well as flavoring to specific cooking and baking recipes.

Flavorings that are labeled "artificial" often have a very artificial taste—and they will add this unfortunate element to your food. These days, it's so easy to find real versions of everyday flavorings like vanilla and almond extract that it's worth a little extra cost—especially as they can often be used in place of more rare flavorings. Before using a new flavor, it's best to taste a few drops because, good or bad, it will affect the food you're making.

CONDIMENTS, SAUCES, AND SPICE MIXTURES

Many of the most common condiments can be easily put together from a few items already in your refrigerator or pantry. That means that, with this book, you won't have a problem when you just get back from shopping only to realize you forgot something like mustard or ketchup.

Perhaps you're a person who likes to amaze your friends with exotic recipes every weekend. There's no need to purchase a shelf full of costly, specialty seasonings you'll only use once before the expiration date. Throughout the book, you'll find guidelines for everything from ordinary sauces to intriguing spice mixtures. Recipes will appear throughout the book in recipe card boxes, such as the following:

With these recipes, you can simply make up a small amount of a familiar condiment as needed, or you can opt for adventure and try something new!

EQUIVALENTS

To make a pie, you need to know how many apples to buy when your recipe calls for pounds rather than an exact quantity of apples. For a stew, you need to know how many potatoes and carrots to peel when the recipe calls for cups. How many lemons do you need to make a tablespoon of juice? Within the main A to Z reference section, you'll find measured equivalents for common fruits, vegetables, and other familiar ingredients.

MEASUREMENTS, METRIC EQUIVALENTS, AND TEMPERATURES

Whether you don't have the right size baking pan, you're trying to remember how many teaspoons are in a tablespoon, or you're converting to or from metric measurements and temperatures, you'll find all the charts you need at the back of this book.

Substituting Ingredients A to Z

Abalone
= clams
= scallops
Note: Cooking times may vary.
See Shellfish

Achiote, also known as annatto seed
= turmeric
= saffron

Acorn squash
See Squash, winter

Adzuki beans, also known as Chinese red beans
= bean paste (miso) or bean curd (tofu)

Agar-agar, 1 tablespoon
   = 4 tablespoons gelatin
   = 3 tablespoons Carrageenan or Irish moss

Ajwan
   = thyme
   = fennel seed
   = caraway seed

Alaskan king crab, also known as king crab
   See Crab

Alfalfa sprouts
   = watercress
   See Sprouts

Allspice, 1 teaspoon
   = ground cloves with cinnamon and nutmeg to taste, in baking
   = black pepper, in cooking

Almond milk
   = soy milk
   Note: Mix with cornstarch if needed for thickening, adding ¼ teaspoon at a time.

Almonds
1 lb. shelled = 1 to 1½ cups
1 lb. in shells = 3½ cups

Amaranth
= chard
= kale with a dash of lemon juice or vinegar
= sorrel
See Greens

Amber cup squash
See Squash, winter

Anchovies
= salt cod, prepared
= herring
= salted fish

Anchovy paste, 1 teaspoon
= 2 anchovy fillets
= 1 teaspoon soy sauce plus 1 teaspoon dulse or kelp flakes

Angel hair pasta
See Pasta

Angostura Bitters

YIELDS ABOUT ⅛ CUP

Mix pinches of cinnamon, cloves, mace, and nutmeg, with finely diced orange and/or lemon peel and prunes, in 2 tablespoons vodka or rum.

Note: The actual formula for Angostura Bitters is secret.

Anise
= fennel

= tarragon

= chervil (use up to twice amount)

Anise, green
= fennel seed

Anise seed
= star anise

= fennel seed

= caraway seed (use 1½ times the amount)

= chervil (use twice the amount)

Apple cider vinegar, also known as cider vinegar
See Vinegar

Apples
1 lb. = 2 large apples
1 lb. = 2 ½ to 3 sliced cups

Apples, chopped, 1 cup
= 1 cup firm pears, chopped, with up to 1 tablespoon lemon
   juice if needed for tart flavor

Apples, sweet/mild
Cortland
Fuji
Gala
Golden delicious
Jonagold
Red delicious
Rome
Russet

Apples, tart
Baldwin
Granny Smith
Gravenstein
Northern Spy

Apples, tart/sweet
Braeburn
Empire

Greening
Honeycrisp
Ida Red
Jazz
Jonathan
Macoun
McIntosh
Pippin
Winesap

Arrowroot, 1 tablespoon
= 1½ tablespoon cornstarch, do not overstir
= 2 tablespoons flour; up to a few tablespoons can be used
  for thickening
= brown rice flour
See Flour

Artichoke hearts
= chayote, cooked
= Jerusalem artichoke, also known as sunchoke
= kohlrabi, cooked

Arugula, also known as rocket
= Belgian endive
= endive
= escarole
= dandelion greens

Asafetida

= equal parts onion powder, celery seed, curry powder, and cumin

Asian fish sauce

See Nam pla

Asian pears

= pears

= atemoya

= cherimoya

= custard apple

Aubergine, also known as eggplant

See Eggplant

Australian blue squash

See Squash, winter

Autumn cup squash

See Squash, winter

Azafran, also known as saffron

See Saffron

Baby carrots

See Carrots, baby

Bacon, up to ½ cup

= smoked ham, in cooking

= ham

Baking powder, 1 teaspoon double-acting

= ½ teaspoon cream of tartar plus ¼ teaspoon baking soda

= ¼ teaspoon baking soda plus ½ cup sour milk or cream or buttermilk; reduce some other liquid from recipe

= ¼ teaspoon baking soda plus 2 more eggs if recipe calls for sweet milk; reduce some other liquid from recipe

= 4 teaspoons quick-cooking tapioca

Baking soda, up to 1 teaspoon

= baking powder plus an acidic ingredient in the recipe, such as buttermilk, sour cream, or citrus (use equal amount baking powder if the recipe contains an acidic ingredient such as buttermilk, sour cream, or citrus; if the recipe does not contain an acidic ingredient, add equal amounts of acidic ingredients)

Balsamic vinegar

See Vinegar

Bamboo leaves

= parchment paper

Note: Neither bamboo leaves nor parchment paper are edible.

Banana squash

See Squash, winter

Bananas
1 lb. = 3 to 4 whole
1 lb. = 2 cups, mashed

Barbecue Sauce
YIELDS 2½ CUPS

½ cup vinegar

1 cup ketchup

½ cup onion, chopped

½ teaspoon cayenne pepper

½ cup brown sugar

2 teaspoons dry mustard

2 tablespoons Worcestershire sauce

½ cup vegetable oil

Continued on next page

½ teaspoon salt (optional)

2 tablespoons liquid smoke (optional)

Combine ingredients. Simmer for 30 minutes, if desired.

Barley, pearl
See Barley, whole
See Grains

Barley, whole
= farro
= spelt
= wheat berries
See Grains

Basil, dried
= oregano
= parsley
= summer savory
= thyme

Basil, lemon
= basil

Basil, mint
= shiso

Basmati rice

= long-grain white rice

Batata

See Boniato

Bay leaf

= thyme

Beach plum

= crab apple

= quince

Beans

The following beans and legumes, or pulses, can be substituted for each other. Cooking times and yields will vary.

= adzuki

= black

= black-eyed pea

= chickpea, also known as garbanzo

= fava

= garbanzo, also known as chickpea

= great northern, also known as white, navy, or pea

= kidney, also known as red

= lentil

= marrow

= mung

= navy, also known as great northern, pea, or white
= pea, also known as great northern, navy, or white
= peas, split
= pinto
= soybean
= white, also known as great northern, navy, or pea

Beans, dried
1 lb. = 1½ to 2 cups
1 lb. = 5 to 6 cups cooked
1 cup = 2 to 2½ cups canned

Beans, green
See Green beans

Bean sprouts
= celery
See Sprouts

Bean thread, also known as cellophane noodles and vermicelli (soybean)
See Noodles, Asian

Beef, ground
= ground turkey
= ground pork
= ground veal

= ground lamb

= chopped, firm tofu

Note: Combinations of beef and these substitutes can also be used in most recipes.

Beet greens

See Greens

Belgian endive

= fennel

See Lettuce and salad greens

Bell peppers

See Peppers

Bergamot

= orange flavoring with a dash of lavender, to taste

Bermuda onions

See Onions, sweet

Berries

1 pint berries = approximately 2 cups

Berries, up to 1 cup in a recipe

Note: Up to 1 cup in a recipe, may be omitted. You may change the flavor of the dish completely, but it may be just as delicious!

= blackberries
= black raspberries
= blueberries
= boysenberries
= cloudberries
= dewberries
= elderberries
= huckleberries
= loganberries
= marionberries
= olallieberries
= raspberries
= salmonberries
= youngberries

Blackberries

See Berries

Black kale, also known as Tuscan kale

See Greens

Black pepper

= white pepper
= allspice in cooking, especially if salt is used in dish

Black peppercorns

= white peppercorns

= pink peppercorns
Note: Peppercorns vary in strength.

Black sesame seed
See Sesame

Blueberries
See Berries

Blue crab
See Crab

Bok choy, also known as pak choi or Chinese cabbage
= Napa cabbage
= Savoy cabbage
= green cabbage

Boletus mushrooms, also known as cèpe or porcini mushrooms
= shiitake mushrooms

Boniato, also known as batata or white sweet potatoes
= sweet potatoes
= yams
= plantains

Borage
= cucumber, especially in dishes with yogurt

Bouquet Garni

= 3 sprigs parsley, 1 sprig thyme, 1 bay leaf

Optional: 1 sprig each of basil, celery leaf, fennel, marjoram,
or tarragon.

Tie sprigs together with string, or tie up in cheesecloth.

Bourbon

= whiskey

Boysenberries

= blackberries

= raspberries

See Berries

Brandy

= cognac

= whiskey

Bread

1 lb. = 10 to 14 slices

1 slice = ½ cup soft breadcrumbs

1 slice = ¼ to ⅓ cup dry breadcrumbs

Breadcrumbs, dry, ¼ cup

= ¼ cup cracker crumbs

= ½ slice bread, cubed, toasted, and crumbled

= ¼ cup instant rolled oats

= ⅓ cup soft breadcrumbs

= $1/4$ cup matzah meal

= $1/4$ cup flour

= $1/4$ cup crushed corn flakes

= $1/4$ cup panko

Breadfruit

= papaya

= winter squash

Broccoli

= broccoli Romanesco, also known as baby green cauliflower

Broccoli rabe, also known as rapini

See Greens

Broth, beef, 1 cup

= 1 beef bouillon cube plus 1 cup water

= 1 cup beef stock

= 1 cup beef consommé

Broth, chicken, 1 cup

= 1 chicken bouillon cube plus 1 cup water

= 1 cup chicken stock

Brussels sprouts

= green cabbage

= Savoy cabbage

= Chinese cabbage

Buckwheat groats, also known as kasha
See Grains

Bulgur
= cracked wheat

= buckwheat or kasha

= brown rice

= couscous

= millet

= quinoa

See Grains

Burdock (root), also known as gobo
= parsnip

Butter
1 lb. = 4 sticks

1 lb. = 2 cups

1 cup = 2 sticks

1 stick = ½ cup

2 tablespoons = ¼ stick

2 tablespoons = 1 ounce

4 tablespoons = ½ stick

4 tablespoons = 2 ounces

8 tablespoons = 1 stick

8 tablespoons = 4 ounces

16 tablespoons = 2 sticks

16 tablespoons = 8 ounces

Butter, 1 cup

= 1⅓ cups whipped

= 1 cup margarine

= ⅞ cup vegetable shortening

= ⅞ cup lard

= ⅞ cup vegetable oil such as canola, corn, cottonseed, or safflower

= ⅞ cup nut oil

= ⅔ cup chicken fat (not for baking or sweets)

= ⅞ cup solid shortening

Note: For softened butter or to stretch butter, blend ½ cup vegetable oil into 1 lb. butter; refrigerate.

Butter, Clarified

YIELDS ⅓ CUP

½ cup butter

Heat butter in a saucepan on low heat for at least 10 minutes. Skim off foam. Pour yellow liquid carefully into another container, leaving white residue of milk solids in the pan. Discard residue. Tightly cover container of clarified butter and store in refrigerator.

Butter, for frying

= oil

= bacon grease (this will flavor food)

Butter, for baking

= margarine

= shortening

= applesauce (up to ½ cup)

= prune purée (up to ½ cup)

= vegetable oil (up to ½ cup)

Note: Oil is generally not interchangeable with butter in crisp cookies.

Buttercup squash

See Squash, winter

Buttermilk, 1 cup

= 1 cup milk plus 2 teaspoons cream of tartar

= 1 cup sour cream

= ½ cup plain, low-fat yogurt plus ½ cup milk

= 1 cup plain, low-fat yogurt

Butternut squash

See Squash, winter

Button mushrooms, also known as market mushrooms

See Mushrooms, market

C

Cabbage
1 lb. = 4 cups shredded raw
1 lb. = 2 cups cooked

Cabbage
See Chinese cabbage, green cabbage, red cabbage, Savoy cabbage

Cactus, also known as nopal
= green pepper
= okra

Cactus pears
= kiwi
= watermelon

Cajun Seasoning
YIELDS ABOUT 1 CUP

2 teaspoons cayenne (or paprika for a milder version)

2 teaspoons thyme

2 teaspoons oregano

1 teaspoon cumin

1 teaspoon mustard powder

Continued on next page

1 teaspoon ground black pepper
2 cloves garlic
1 onion
2 teaspoons salt

Mix in a food processor or with a mortar and pestle.

Cake flour
See Flour

Calabazo, also known as West Indian pumpkin or Cuban squash
See Squash, winter

Calamari, also known as squid
= octopus or baby octopus

Callaloo
= spinach
= chard
= turnip greens
See Greens

Capers
= chopped green olives
= pickled green nasturtium seeds

Capiscum
See Peppers, green or bell
See Peppers, yellow
See Peppers, red, sweet

Capon
= large roasting chicken

Carambola, also known as starfruit
See Starfruit

Caraway seed
= fennel seed
= cumin seed

Cardamom
= cinnamon
= mace

Cardoni, also known as cardoon
See Cardoon

Cardoon, also known as cardoni or wild artichoke
= artichoke heart

Carnival squash
See Squash, winter

Carrageenan, also known as Irish moss, 2 tablespoons
= 1 envelope or 1 tablespoon gelatin
= 2 teaspoons agar

Carrots
= parsnips

Carrots
1 lb. = 3 cups sliced raw
1 lb. = 4 cups shredded

Carrots, baby
= carrots

Cassava, also known as manioc or yuca
= sweet potato
= yam

Cassia
= cinnamon

Caster sugar
See Sugar, superfine

Cauliflower
= kohlrabi

Cayenne pepper

= hot red pepper, ground

= chili powder

Celeriac, also known as celery root

= parsnip (cooked)

= jicama (raw)

= celery

Celery
1 medium stalk = ⅓ cup diced

Celery

= green pepper

= jicama

= bean sprouts

= Belgian endive

= fennel

= lovage stalks

Celery root, also known as celeriac

See Celeriac

Celery salt, 1 teaspoon

= ¾ teaspoon salt plus ¼ teaspoon ground or crushed celery seed

Celery seed
= dill seed

Cellophane noodles, also known as bean thread and vermicelli (soybean)
See Noodles, Asian

Cèpes, also known as porcini or boletus mushrooms
= shiitake mushrooms

Champagne vinegar
See Vinegar

Chanterelle mushrooms
= pied de mouton or hedgehog mushrooms

Chard, Swiss
See Greens

Chayote squash, also known as mirliton or christophine squash
See Squash, summer

Cheese
4 oz. = 1 cup shredded

Cheese

Within each group, cheeses can be substituted for each other.

American
Cheddar
Cheshire
Colby
Edam
Fontina
Gouda
Havarti
Longhorn
Monterey Jack
Muenster
Port-Salut
***

Blue (also known as bleu) cheese
Cambozola
Gorgonzola
Maytag
Roquefort
Stilton
***

Emmenthaler
Gruyère
Jarlsberg
Raclette
Swiss
***

Mozzarella (for cooking, not buffalo mozzarella)
Provolone
***
Brie
Camembert
***
Asiago, aged
Grana padano
Parmesan
Pecorino
Pecorino Romano
Romano
***
Cottage cheese
Cream cheese
Farmer cheese
Hoop cheese
Mascarpone
Ricotta
Yogurt (especially in dips)

Cheese, cottage

See Cottage cheese
See Cheeses

Cheeses

BLOOMY-RIND OR EDIBLE-RIND
Brie

Camembert
Taleggio

FRESH AND MILD

Buffalo mozzarella
Cottage cheese
Farmer's cheese
Hoop cheese
Mascarpone
Ricotta

FRESH AND PUNGENT

Chèvre, also known as goat cheese
Feta
Goat cheese, also known as chèvre

WASHED-RIND

Muenster
Pont l'Eveque

SEMI-SOFT (SEMI-HARD)

Havarti
Livarot

PRESSED

Cheddar
Cheshire
Edam

Gouda
Jarlsberg
Mozzarella
Swiss

AGED

Asiago, aged
Grana padano
Parmesan
Pecorino
Pecorina Roman
Romano

BLUE

Cambozola
Gorgonzola
Maytag
Roquefort
Stilton

Cheese Topping for Popcorn

YIELDS ABOUT ½ CUP

¼ cup Parmesan cheese
¼ cup grated blue cheese

Continued on next page

1 teaspoon paprika

½ teaspoon garlic powder

½ teaspoon onion powder or onion salt

Sprinkle on popped popcorn. Warm briefly in microwave
or oven before serving.

Cherimoya
= sweetsop

= guanabana, also known as soursop

= atemoya

= pears, pineapples, and bananas in equal amounts, with a
dash of lemon or lime juice

= melons and peaches

= guavas and peaches

Cherries, red
= Rainier cherries

Chervil
= tarragon (use ½ the amount)

= anise (use ½ the amount)

= Italian parsley

Chicken breasts, boneless
= turkey breast slices

= veal scallops

Chicken pieces

= turkey

= Cornish game hen

= squab

= quail

= rabbit

Chicory

= endive

= sorrel

See Lettuce and salad greens

Chile peppers

See Chili peppers

Chili Oil, also known as Red Pepper Oil

YIELDS ABOUT ⅛ CUP

3 tablespoons sesame oil

3 to 4 small spicy red peppers

Heat oil. Fry peppers until they turn dark, but do not burn.
Remove peppers and discard. Use the remaining oil.

Chili paste

See Sambal

Chili pepper, hot, also known as chili powder
See Chili powder

Chili peppers, hot or milder
See Peppers, chili

Chili Powder

YIELDS 2 TO 3 TEASPOONS

$^1/_2$ teaspoon cumin

$^1/_2$ teaspoon dried oregano

$^1/_4$ teaspoon black pepper

$^1/_4$ teaspoon cayenne pepper

$^1/_4$ teaspoon chopped garlic

$^1/_4$ teaspoon cilantro

$^1/_4$ teaspoon paprika

Optional: Turmeric, white pepper, finely chopped lemon peel, cardamom

Mix well.

Chinese broccoli
See Greens

Chinese cabbage
= cabbage
= lettuce

Chinese parsley, also known as cilantro or coriander leaf
See Cilantro

Chinese red beans, also known as adzuki beans
See Adzuki beans

Chives
= green onion tops
= onion powder (use ⅛ amount)
= leeks
= shallots (use ¼ amount)
See Onions

Chocolate, baking
1 square = 1 oz.

Chocolate, baking, unsweetened, 1 ounce
= 3 tablespoons unsweetened cocoa plus 1 tablespoon butter or margarine
= 3 tablespoons carob powder plus 2 tablespoons water

Chocolate, baking, unsweetened, premelted, 1 ounce
= 3 tablespoons unsweetened cocoa plus 1 tablespoon oil or melted shortening

Chocolate, Mexican
YIELDS 3 OUNCES

3 ounces semisweet chocolate

1 teaspoon cinnamon

½ teaspoon almond or vanilla extract

1 tablespoon sugar (unless unsweetened chocolate is specified for recipe)

Melt together, mix, and cool.

Chocolate, Semisweet
YIELDS 6 OUNCES

9 tablespoons unsweetened cocoa powder

7 tablespoons sugar

3 tablespoons butter

Chocolate, white
= white icing for drizzling

= other flavored chips for sweet desserts

Chocolate chips or morsels
1 12-oz. package = 2 cups

Choy sum, also known as flowering cabbage
= bok choi, also known as pak choy

Christophine squash, also known as chayote or mirliton squash

See Squash, sumner

Chutney

YIELDS ABOUT 1½ CUPS

1 8-ounce jar apricot or peach preserves

1 clove garlic, minced, or ½ teaspoon garlic powder

½ teaspoon powdered ginger, or 1 tablespoon fresh or candied ginger, minced

½ teaspoon salt

1 tablespoon apple cider vinegar

½ cup raisins (optional)

Warm preserves to lukewarm. Mix in remainder of ingredients.

Ciabatta bread

= baked pizza dough

= focaccia bread

Cider vinegar, also known as apple cider vinegar

See Vinegar

Cilantro, also known as coriander leaf or Chinese parsley

= parsley with a dash of lemon juice

= orange peel with a pinch of sage

= lemon grass with a pinch of mint

= parsley and mint in equal amounts

= Italian parsley (for garnish)

Cinnamon

= cardamom with ⅛ amount allspice or nutmeg

= ¼ amount allspice

= ¼ amount nutmeg

Cipollini

= wild onions

Clams

= cockles

= mussels

= oysters

Note: Canned clams with some of their liquid can be used
      in cooking.

See Shellfish

Clementines

= mandarin oranges

= tangerines

= satsumas

= oranges

Cloudberries
See Berries

Cloves, ground
= allspice

= nutmeg

= mace

Club soda
= mineral water

= seltzer

Coarse salt
= Kosher salt

= sea salt

Cockles
= small clams

Cocktail Sauce
YIELDS ABOUT 1 CUP
2 tablespoons horseradish
½ cup ketchup
1½ teaspoons Worcestershire sauce (optional)
2 tablespoons lemon juice (optional)
black pepper (optional)

Continued on next page

bottled hot sauce (to taste; optional)

¹/₄ cup chili sauce (optional)

Combine ingredients.

Cocoa, hot, instant mix

YIELDS DRY MIX TO MAKE 1 CUP COCOA

³/₄ cup instant nonfat dry milk

2 tablespoons sugar

2 tablespoons cocoa

Stir together.

Cocoa powder, for baking, ¼ cup

= ¹/₂ cup semisweet chocolate chips

Coconut, grated

Note: If less than ¹/₂ cup, can be omitted from recipe.

Coconut milk, fresh, thick, 1 cup

= ¹/₂ cup fresh chopped coconut plus ¹/₂ cup water, bring to boil, let stand for 1 hour to infuse

= 4 to 5 tablespoons coconut cream, solidified, dissolved in 1 cup hot water or milk

= 1 cup top layer canned cream of coconut liquid

= 1 cup medium cream with 1 teaspoon coconut flavoring

Coconut milk, fresh, thin, 1 cup
= 2 tablespoons (solidified) coconut cream, dissolved in 1 cup hot water or milk
= 1 cup canned cream of coconut liquid
= 1 cup whole milk with 1 teaspoon coconut flavoring
= 1 cup milk blended with 3 tablespoons grated coconut

Coffee

$\frac{1}{2}$ cup strong brewed =
1 teaspoon instant in $\frac{1}{2}$ cup water
1 lb. ground = 80 tablespoons
1 lb. ground = 30 to 40 servings

Cognac
= brandy
= whiskey

Collard greens
See Greens

Condensed Milk, Sweetened
YIELDS ABOUT ½ CUP

1 cup instant powdered milk
⅓ cup hot water
½ cup sugar
1 tablespoon melted butter or margarine

Blend ingredients until dissolved and smooth.

Coriander leaf, also known as Chinese parsley or cilantro
See Cilantro

Coriander seed
= caraway with a dash of cumin

= lemon zest with a dash of sage

= allspice with a pinch of lemon or lemon zest

Corn
6 ears = 2 to 3 cups kernels

Corn flour
= flour, up to a few tablespoons, for thickening

See Flour

Cornish game hen
= squab

= quail

= chicken

Cornmeal
= (corn) grits

= masa harina

= polenta

See Grains

Cornstarch, 1 tablespoon

= 2 tablespoons flour

= 1 tablespoon arrowroot

= 2 tablespoons quick-cooking tapioca

= 2 eggs

See Flour

Corn syrup, dark, 1 cup

= ¾ cup light corn syrup plus ¼ cup molasses

= ¾ cup golden syrup plus ¼ cup molasses

= 1¼ cups brown sugar plus ⅓ cup liquid boiled down to 1 cup. You can use any liquid from the recipe you are making—if there is no liquid in the recipe, add ⅓ cup water and boil down to 1 cup.

Corn syrup, light, 1 cup

= 1 cup golden syrup

= 1¼ cups sugar plus ⅓ cup water or other liquid from recipe, boiled down to 1 cup

Cos

See Lettuce and salad greens

Cottage cheese

1 lb. = 2 cups

Cottage cheese

= ricotta cheese

= soft tofu

See Cheeses

Courgettes, also known as zucchini

See Squash, summer

Couscous

= orzo

= quinoa

= white rice

= bulgur

= kasha

= millet

= brown rice

= tabouleh

= cracked wheat

= wheat berries

Couscous, Israeli, also known as pearl couscous

See Couscous

Crab

The following crab meats can be substituted for each other:
Alaskan king crab, also known as king crab
Blue crab

Dungeness crab
Jonah crab
King crab, also known as Alaskan king crab
Softshell crab
Stone crab
See Shellfish

Crabmeat, fresh (cooked)

= use frozen crabmeat (not canned) for true flavor
See Shellfish

Cranberries

= quince
= sour cherries

Crayfish

= langouste
= langoustine
= lobster
= prawns
= shrimp
See Shellfish

Cream, clotted, also known as Devonshire cream

= heavy cream, whipped to soft peaks
= sour cream with a pinch of baking soda
= crème fraîche

Cream, heavy, not for whipping, 1 cup
= ¾ cup milk plus ¼ cup shortening or butter
= ⅔ cup evaporated milk

Cream, heavy or whipping
1 cup = 2 cups whipped

Cream, light (or half-and-half), 1 cup
= ½ cup heavy cream plus ½ cup milk
= ⅞ cup milk plus 3 tablespoons butter or margarine
= ½ cup evaporated milk plus ½ cup milk

Cream, whipped, sweetened, 1 cup
= 1 4-ounce package frozen whipped topping
= 1 envelope whipped topping mix, prepared as directed
= 1 mashed banana beaten with 1 stiffly beaten egg white plus 1 teaspoon sugar
= 1 cup nonfat dry milk powder whipped with 1 cup ice water and sweetened to taste (this is for low-calorie desserts and drinks; it will not hold for long)
= 1 cup ice-cold evaporated milk, plus 2 teaspoons sugar, whipped (use immediately)

Cream cheese
= cottage cheese blended with cream; add butter and/or milk to correct consistency
= Neufchatel cheese

Cream of tartar
= lemon juice or vinegar, when used for stabilizing beaten egg whites

Crème fraîche
= sour cream, in recipes
= ½ sour cream and ½ heavy cream

Crème Fraîche
YIELDS 1½ CUPS
1 cup heavy cream
½ cup buttermilk or sour cream or sour milk or yogurt
Stir well in glass container. To make firm crème fraîche, let sit in a warm place for 6 hours. Refrigerate if not using immediately.

Crosnes
= Jerusalem artichoke
= jicama

Cuban squash, also known as calabazo or West Indian pumpkin
See Squash, winter

Cumin

= caraway and anise combined, to taste

= fennel seed

Currants, fresh

=ground cherries

= gooseberries

= sour cherries

Currants, dried

= raisins

= soft prunes or dates, finely chopped

Note: If less than ¼ cup, can be omitted from recipe.

Curry Powder

YIELDS ABOUT ⅔ CUP

2 tablespoons ground coriander

2 tablespoons cumin

2 tablespoons red pepper

2 tablespoons turmeric

2 tablespoons ground ginger

Optional: Dash of some of the following: allspice, black pepper, cinnamon, ground fennel, fenugreek, garlic powder, mace, mustard powder

Combine all ingredients.

Custard apple
= cherimoya

= sweetsop

= atemoya

= soursop, also known as guanabana

Daikon
= jicama

= radish

Dandelion greens
See Lettuce and salad greens

Dasheen, also known as taro
See Taro

Dashi
= light fish stock

Dates
1 lb. = 2 cups chopped, pitted

Dates

= raisins

= figs

= prunes

Note: If less than ½ cup, can be omitted from recipe.

Delicata squash

= *See Squash, winter*

Devonshire cream, also known as clotted cream

See Cream, clotted

Dewberries

See Berries

Dill seed

= caraway seed

= celery seed

Duck Sauce, also known as Plum Sauce

YIELDS ABOUT ¼ CUP

¼ cup apricot jelly or plum jelly

1 teaspoon vinegar

1 to 1½ teaspoons sugar

Stir until sugar dissolves.

Dungeness crab
See Crab

Edamame, also known as soy beans
= lima beans
= broad beans
= fava beans

Edible blossoms, for garnishes and in salads
bachelor buttons
blue borage
borage
calendula petals
chive blossoms
dandelion
daylily
dianthus
hollyhock
Johnny-jump-ups, also known as violas
lavender
marigold petals
mini carnations
nasturtiums

pansies

rocket

rose petals

snapdragons

sweet pea

violas, also known as Johnny-jump-ups

wild radish

Eggplant, also known as aubergine

= large zucchini

Eggs

1 cup = 4 to 5 large

1 cup = 8 to 10 whites

1 cup = 10 to 12 yolks

Eggs, for scrambling

= tofu, lightly chopped

Eggs, whole

= 2 tablespoons liquid plus 2 tablespoons flour plus ½ tablespoon shortening plus ½ teaspoon baking powder

= 2 yolks plus 1 tablespoon water

= 2 yolks, in custards, sauces, or similar mixtures

= 2 tablespoons oil plus 1 tablespoon water

= 1 teaspoon cornstarch plus 3 tablespoons more liquid in recipe

Note: If halving recipe, do not try to halve one egg; use one whole egg. If short one more egg in recipe, substitute 1 teaspoon vinegar or 1 teaspoon baking powder and 2 tablespoons more liquid.

Elderberries

See Berries

Elephant garlic

= garlic (use ½ amount or to taste)

Endive, also known as curly endive

= Belgian endive

= chicory

= escarole

See Lettuce and salad greens

Enoki, also known as enokitake mushrooms

= oyster mushrooms

Enokitake, also known as enoki mushrooms

See Enoki

Escarole

= arugula

= endive

= chicory (use ½ amount)

= sorrel (use ¼ amount)
See Greens

Evaporated milk
= light cream or half-and-half
= heavy cream

Farina, quick cooking
See Grains

Farro
= spelt
= barley
= wheat berries
See Grains

Fava beans
= lima beans, especially baby lima beans

Feijoa
See Pineapple guava

Fennel bulb, also known as Florentine fennel
= Belgian endive
= celery

Fennel seed
= caraway seed
= anise, also known as anise seed
= star anise

Fenugreek
= celery seed
= lovage

Fiddlehead ferns
1 lb. = 2⅔ cups chopped
Note: If less than ½ cup, can be
omitted from recipe.

Fiddlehead ferns
See Greens

Figs
1 lb. = 2⅔ cups chopped
Note: If less than ½ cup, can be
omitted from recipe.

Figs

Black mission
Brown Turkey
Calimyrna
Kadota
Panchee, also known as tiger fig
Tiger fig, also known as panchee
Note: These are equivalent in recipes.

Filé powder, also known as gumbo filé or sassafras

See Sassafras

Fines Herbes
YIELDS ABOUT 1½ TABLESPOONS
1 teaspoon parsley
1 teaspoon tarragon
1 teaspoon chervil
1 teaspoon chives
Mince together.

Fish (varieties)

Alaska cod, also known Pacific cod or gray cod
bass, also known as branzino
black cod, also known as sablefish
branzino, also known as bass

dorade, also known as sea bream
hamachi, also known as yellowtail
lotte, also known as monkfish
loup de mer, also known as sea bass
monkfish, also known as lotte
ono, also known as wahoo
opakapaka, also known as pink snapper rock shrimp
sablefish, also known as black cod
sea bass, also known as loup de mer
sea bream, also known as dorade
snapper, also known as vivaneau
vivaneau, also known as snapper
wahoo, also known as ono
yellowtail, also known as hamachi

Fish, fillets

bass
bluefish
carp
catfish
Chilean sea bass, also known as Patagonian toothfish
cod
coho salmon, also known as salmon trout
dorade, also known as sea bream
flounder
fluke
grouper

haddock

hake

halibut

John Dory

ling cod

loup de mer, also known as sea bass

mahi mahi

monkfish, also known as lotte

muskellunge, also known as muskie

muskie, also known as muskellunge

nilefish

orange roughy

pickerel

pike

plaice

pollock

red snapper

rock cod

rockfish

salmon

salmon trout, also known as coho salmon

sandab

scrod (this is a type of catch, not a type of fish)

sea bass, also known as loup de mer

sea bass, Chilean

sea bream, also known as dorade

shark (dogfish)

sole
striped bass
talapia, also known as St. Peter's fish
trout
turbot
walleyed pike
whitefish
yellow croaker

Fish, steaks

ahi
albacore
catfish
cod
halibut
John Dory
mackerel
mahi mahi
oono, also known as wahoo
salmon
sea bass
shark
sturgeon
swordfish
tilefish
tuna
wahoo, also known as oono

Fish, whole

bass

catfish

flounder

halibut

mackerel

muskellunge, also known as muskie

perch

pike

salmon

sardines

smelt

trout

turbot

yellow croaker

Fish sauce (Asian)

See Nam pla

Five-Spice Powder
YIELDS ABOUT 1 TABLESPOON
1 teaspoon ground star anise
1 teaspoon ground fennel seed
1 teaspoon ground Szechwan pepper
½ teaspoon ground cassia or cinnamon
½ teaspoon ground cloves
Stir together.

Flavored vinegar

See Vinegar

Flavorings (extracts and aromatics)

Commonly available; some are imitation:

almond

anise

banana

brandy

butter

cherry

chocolate

coconut

lemon

liquid smoke

maple

mint

orange

peppermint

pineapple

root beer

rose water

rum

vanilla

See Liqueurs

Fleur de sel

= sea salt

Florentine fennel

See Fennel

Flour

1 lb. white = 3½ to 4 cups

1 cup white = 4 ounces, approximately

1 cup white = 1 cup plus 2 tablespoons cake flour
(and omit up to 2 tablespoons cornstarch if in recipe)

1 lb. cake = 4 to 4½ cups

1 cup cake = ⅞ cup white flour

1 lb. whole wheat = 3 cups sifted (do not overmix)

Flour, cake, 1 cup

= 2 tablespoons cornstarch plus ⅞ cup flour

Flour, for thickening, up to a few tablespoons only

= Bisquick

= tapioca, quick cooking

= cornstarch or corn flour (smaller amounts may be required)

= arrowroot (smaller amounts may be required)

= brown rice flour

= soy flour

= rye flour

= potato flour

= potato starch

= mashed potatoes, flakes or prepared

= 1 whole egg or 2 yolks or 2 whites (especially for cooked sauces; whisk continuously while adding)

= pancake mix, for coating pork chops or chicken

Flour, graham

= whole wheat flour

Flour, self-rising, 1 cup

= 1 cup flour plus ¼ teaspoon baking powder

Optional: Add a pinch of salt

Flour, white, for baking, 1 cup

= 1 cup plus 2 tablespoons cake flour

= ¾ cup whole wheat flour; reduce shortening to ⅔ the amount for cookies; add 1 or 2 more tablespoons liquid for cakes; add more liquid for bread.

Note: Whole wheat flour will make the product denser (heavier); it's advisable to start out substituting half whole wheat or other grain flours. Rye, for instance, has a nutty flavor. Soy can also be used for extra protein; substitute ⅒ to ¼ soy flour for wheat flour.

Flour, whole wheat, 1 cup

= 1 cup graham flour

= 2 tablespoons wheat germ plus enough white flour to make 1 cup.

Note: Product may be less dense or lighter when using white flour.

Flowers, for garnishes and in salads
See Edible blossoms

Focaccia bread
= baked pizza dough
= ciabatta bread

Fuzzy melon, also known as hairy cucumber
= zucchini

Galangal, also known as Laos powder
= ginger root
= powdered ginger with a dash of cardamom

Garam Masala
YIELDS ⅓ CUP
2 teaspoons ground cardamom
4 teaspoons ground cumin
1 teaspoon ground cloves
2 teaspoons black pepper
1 teaspoon ground cinnamon
1 teaspoon ground nutmeg

Continued on next page

Optional pinch of ginger, coriander, or both

Combine.

Garlic
1 clove garlic = ½ to 1 teaspoon chopped garlic

Garlic, 1 clove
- = ½ teaspoon minced, dried garlic
- = ¼ teaspoon garlic powder
- = ¼ teaspoon garlic juice
- = ½ teaspoon garlic salt (and omit ½ teaspoon salt from recipe)
- = garlic chives (use up to 4 times amount)
- = elephant garlic (use up to twice amount)

Garlic, green
- = leeks

Garlic Butter
YIELDS ¼ CUP

1 clove garlic
4 tablespoons salted butter, softened

Peel the garlic clove, then pound or mash it. Add butter, and mix well. Add ¼ teaspoon salt if butter is unsalted.

Gelatin, 1 tablespoon or 1 envelope

= 2 teaspoons agar

= 2 tablespoons carrageenan or Irish moss

Ghee

= clarified butter

Ginger, fresh, grated

= powdered ginger (about ¼ amount) with a dash of white pepper and lemon juice

= minced, crystallized ginger with sugar washed off

Ginger, powdered

= grated fresh ginger

= mace with a pinch of lemon peel

= nutmeg (about ¼ the amount)

Gold pepper, also known as yellow pepper

See Yellow pepper

Golden nugget squash

See Squash, winter

Golden raisins

See Raisins

Golden syrup

= light corn syrup

= dark corn syrup

Gooseberries

= currants, fresh

= sour cherries

= ground cherries

Grains

Note: These grains (including rice) can be served in place of each other, depending on your taste. Preparation times will vary.

= amaranth

= barley

= barley, pearl

= barley, whole

= buckwheat groats, also known as kasha

= bulgur

= cornmeal

= couscous

= farina

= farro

= grits

= hominy grits

= kasha, also known as buckwheat groats

= millet

= oatmeal
= oats, rolled
= oats, steel-cut
= quinoa
= rice, arborio
= rice, basmati
= rice, brown
= rice, long grain
= rice, short grain
= rice, white
= rye berries
= spelt
= triticale
= wheat, cracked
= wheat berries
= wild rice

Great northern beans

= marrow beans
= navy beans
= pea beans
= white beans
See Beans

Green beans

= haricots verts
= wax beans

Green cabbage
- = Savoy cabbage
- = Chinese cabbage
- = kohlrabi
- = lettuce
- = Brussels sprouts, shredded (especially in cooked dishes)

Green onions, also known as scallions
- = leeks
- = shallots (use ½ amount)
- = chives (use up to twice amount)

Green peppers
See Peppers

Greens, mild in flavor
amaranth
beet greens
bok choy
collard greens
mache
minutina
pea tendrils

Greens, medium in flavor
Belgian endive, also known as witloof
black kale, also known as Tuscan kale

callaloo

chard, also known as Swiss chard

cress

curly endive, also known as escarole

dandelion (young leaves only)

endive

escarole, also known as curly endive

kale

kale, Tuscan, also known as black kale

mizuna

radicchio

spinach

Swiss chard, also known as chard

turnip greens

watercress

witloof, also known as Belgian endive

Greens, strong in flavor

arugula, also known as rocket

broccoli rabe, also known as rapini

chicory

dandelion greens

fiddlehead ferns

mustard greens

nettles (early leaves only)

rapini, also known as broccoli rabe

rocket, also known as arugula

sorrel

tatsoi

turnip greens

Greens, mesclun
= mixture of greens of varying flavors
See Greens

Greens, micro
micro beet

micro mizuna

micro red mustard

micro tatsoi

Grits (corn)
= cornmeal
= polenta

Gros sel
= coarse salt
= kosher salt

Ground cherries
= ripe tomatillos

Grouse
= Cornish game hen

= squab

= quail

Guanabana, also known as soursop

See Soursop

Guava

= pears with a pinch of nutmeg and dash of lime juice

= strawberries, pineapple, and banana, to taste

Gumbo filé, also known as filé powder or sassafras

See Sassafras

Gunga peas

See Pigeon peas

Hairy cucumber, also known as fuzzy melon

See Fuzzy melon

Haricots verts

= young green beans

Harissa Sauce, also known as Tunisian Hot Sauce

YIELDS ABOUT ⅔ CUP

1 whole head of garlic, peeled

6 small red chilies (if dried, soak first)

1 tablespoon ground coriander

1 tablespoon ground cumin

1 tablespoon caraway seeds

1 tablespoon dried mint

1 tablespoon olive oil

1 teaspoon salt

3 tablespoons (or more) fresh coriander

Blend in a food processor.

Hazelnuts

See Nuts

Hedgehog mushrooms, also known as pied de mouton

See Mushrooms

Herb Butter

YIELDS ⅓ CUP

½ teaspoon parsley, chopped

½ teaspoon chives, chopped

½ teaspoon tarragon, chopped

½ teaspoon shallots, chopped

Continued on next page

4 tablespoons salted butter, creamed

Combine.

Herbes de Provence

YIELDS 1 TO 2 TABLESPOONS

1 teaspoon fresh thyme

1 teaspoon fresh summer savory

$\frac{1}{2}$ teaspoon fresh oregano

$\frac{1}{2}$ teaspoon fresh basil

$\frac{1}{4}$ teaspoon fresh rosemary

Mince together. Once prepared, herbs may be used fresh or dried.

Hoisin Sauce

YIELDS ABOUT $\frac{1}{2}$ CUP

3 tablespoons black beans

1 teaspoon garlic powder

3 tablespoons soy sauce

2 tablespoons honey

Put beans in food processor and pulverize. Add rest of ingredients and mix well.

Hominy grits

See Grains

Honey
1 lb. honey = 1⅓ cups honey

Honey, in baking, 1 cup

= corn syrup, light or dark

= molasses

= 1¼ cups sugar plus ¼ cup more liquid

Note: Substitutes may cause the product to brown faster.

Honey Butter
YIELDS ¼ CUP

1 tablespoon honey

3 tablespoons butter, softened

Blend well.

Honey Mustard
YIELDS ¼ CUP

2 tablespoons honey

3 tablespoons prepared yellow mustard

Blend well.

Horseradish, fresh, grated

= daikon radish

= wasabi

Hot Fudge Sauce

YIELDS ABOUT 1½ CUPS

1 egg, slightly beaten

1 cup sugar

¼ cup cream

2 squares unsweetened baking chocolate

1 tablespoon butter

1 teaspoon vanilla

Heat first four ingredients slowly over low heat. Bring to
   a boil. Cool slightly. Beat in butter and vanilla. Serve
   warm.

Hot Fudge Sauce, Bittersweet

YIELDS 2½ CUPS

4 squares unsweetened baking chocolate

3 tablespoons butter

⅔ cup water

1¾ cups sugar

¾ cup corn syrup

1 teaspoon vanilla or rum

Continued on next page

Melt butter and chocolate slowly over low heat. Add water, sugar, and corn syrup. Boil 10 minutes. Allow to cool slightly. Beat in vanilla or rum. Serve warm.

Hot Pepper Jelly

YIELDS 1 CUP

1 cup apple jelly

1½ small, hot chilies or 2 tablespoons canned chili peppers

Combine. Process in a food processor.

Hot pepper sauce

= bottled hot sauce

= Tabasco sauce

= ground red pepper (smaller amounts may be required)

= cayenne pepper (smaller amounts may be required)

= hot red pepper flakes (smaller amounts may be required)

= chili powder (smaller amounts may be required)

Hot red pepper flakes

= chopped, dried red chile peppers

= powdered red chile pepper (smaller amounts may be required)

Hubbard squash

See Squash, winter

Huckleberries
See Berries

Icing sugar
See Sugar, powdered

Irish moss, also known as carrageenan, 2 tablespoons
= 1 envelope or 1 tablespoon gelatin
= 2 teaspoons agar

Israeli couscous
See Couscous

Italian Seasoning
YIELDS ABOUT ¼ CUP

1 tablespoon oregano
1 tablespoon thyme
1 tablespoon basil
1 tablespoon parsley
Optional: Add up to 1 teaspoon marjoram and/or rosemary
Note: All ingredients should be either dried or fresh; do not mix dried and fresh.

Mix together.

Jackfruit
See Breadfruit

Jaggery, 1 cup
= ½ cup white sugar plus ½ cup brown sugar

Japanese pears
See Asian pears

Jerusalem artichokes, also known as sunchokes
= artichoke hearts
= crosnes

Jicama
= crosnes
= daikon
= raw turnip
= water chestnut

Juniper berries
= a small amount of gin, boiled for a few minutes
= bay leaves with a pinch of caraway seeds and chopped mint

Kabocha squash
See Squash, winter

Kale
See Greens

Kale, Tuscan, also known as black kale
= kale

Kasha, also known as buckwheat groats
See Grains

Ketchup I
YIELDS 1 CUP

½ cup tomato sauce

2 tablespoons sugar

2 tablespoons vinegar

½ teaspoon salt

⅛ teaspoon ground cloves

Combine and blend well.

Ketchup II

YIELDS ABOUT 1 CUP

$1/2$ cup tomato sauce
$1/2$ cup tomato paste
$1/4$ cup sugar
3 tablespoons vinegar
1 teaspoon salt

Combine and blend well.

Key limes
= limes (smaller amounts may be required)

Kidney beans
= pink beans
= pinto beans
= red beans

King crab
See Crab

Kiwi fruit
= strawberries with a few dashes of lime juice

Kohlrabi
= cauliflower
= artichoke heart

= broccoli stems
= cabbage
= celeriac
= radish
= turnip

Kosher salt
= coarse salt

Kudzu
= beets

Kumquat
= orange mixed with half the amount of lime, and a dash of bergamot

Langouste
= crayfish
= langoustine
= lobster
= prawns
= shrimp
See Shellfish

Langoustine

= crayfish

= langouste

= lobster

= prawns

= shrimp

See Shellfish

Laos powder, also known as galangal

See Galangal

Leeks

= shallots

= green onions

= ramps

= green garlic

= onions (smaller amounts may be required)

See Onions

Lemon

1 medium lemon = 2 to 3 tablespoons lemon juice
1 medium lemon = 1 tablespoon grated lemon rind (zest)

Lemon, as flavoring

= lime

= lemongrass

= verbena

Lemongrass

= lemon zest

= verbena

= lemon juice

Lemon juice

= lemon peel

= vinegar

= lime juice

= crushed Vitamin C pills mixed with water to taste (for flavoring, up to 1 tablespoon)

Lemon peel, grated, 1 teaspoon

= 2 tablespoons lemon juice

= equal amount of marmalade

= equal amount of lime or orange peel

Note: If less than 1 tablespoon, can be omitted from recipe, especially if another flavoring or essence is used.

See Flavorings

Lemons

= limes

Lentils

= green lentils
= red lentils
= split peas
Note: Preparation and cooking times will vary.

Lettuce and salad greens, buttery and soft

bibb, also known as limestone
Boston, also known as butterhead
butterhead, also known as Boston
corn salad, also known as lamb's lettuce or mâche
green leaf
lamb's lettuce, also known as corn salad or mâche
limestone, also known as bibb
mâche, also known as lamb's lettuce or corn salad
mesclun
oak leaf
red leaf
salad bowl

Lettuce and salad greens, crisp and crunchy

cos, also known as romaine
crisphead, also known as iceberg
iceberg, also known as crisphead
romaine, also known as cos

Lettuce and salad greens, pungent to slightly bitter

arugula, also known as rocket

Belgian endive

chicory, also known as curly endive or friseé

curly endive, also known as chicory or friseé

dandelion greens

escarole

friseé, also known as chicory or curly endive

garden cress, also known as pepper grass

mizuna

mustard greens

nasturtium leaves

pepper grass, also known as garden cress

purslane

radicchio

rocket, also known as arugula

sorrel

watercress

Lima beans
= fava beans

Lime juice
= lemon juice

Limes
1 medium lime = 2 tablespoons juice

Limes

= lemons

Lingonberries

= cranberries

= currants, fresh

Liqueurs

Standard liqueur flavors include:

anise (or licorice): Pastis, Ouzo, Pernod, Arak

black currant: Cassis, Chambord

mint: Crème de Menthe

orange: Curacao, Grand Marnier, Cointreau, Triple Sec

Litchi

See Lychee

Lobster

= crayfish

= langouste

= langoustine

= prawns

= shrimp

See Shellfish

Lobster tail

See Lobster

Loganberries

See Berries

Lo mein

See Noodles, Asian

Lovage

= celery leaves with a dash of curry powder and ground black pepper

= celery leaves

Lychee, also known as litchi

= grapes, peeled

M

Macaroni
1 lb. elbow = 8 to 9 cups cooked

Macaroni

See Pasta, tube

Mace

= allspice

= cloves

= nutmeg
Optional: Add dash of cardamom

Mâche

= arugula
= spinach
See Lettuce and salad greens

Madeira

= sherry
= port
= Marsala
= sweet vermouth

Malt vinegar

See Vinegar

Mandarin oranges

= clementines
= satstumas
= tangerines
= oranges

Mango

= peach with a dash of lemon and allspice

Manioc, also known as yuca or cassava

See Cassava

Maple syrup

See Pancake syrup

Margarine
1 lb. = 4 sticks
1 lb. = 2 cups
1 stick = ½ cup

Margarine

= butter

= shortening

See Butter, in baking

Marinade for Beef, Lamb, or Chicken

YIELDS ABOUT 2½ CUPS

1 cup red wine or red wine vinegar for beef or lamb; or
   1 cup dry white wine for chicken

1 cup salad oil or olive oil or combination

2 cloves garlic

1 teaspoon black pepper, freshly ground

¼ cup minced fresh parsley

½ teaspoon dried thyme

½ teaspoon dried marjoram

Continued on next page

1 bay leaf

Optional: 1 small onion, chopped; 1 small carrot, chopped;
   2 allspice berries, whole; 1 teaspoon salt; ½ teaspoon
   dried rosemary

Combine ingredients.

Marinade for Fish or Chicken

YIELDS ABOUT 3½ CUPS

1½ cups soy sauce

1¾ cups ketchup (optional)

¼ cup dry red wine

2 tablespoons fresh grated ginger

2 tablespoons brown sugar

1 small onion, finely chopped

Juice of 1 lemon (2 to 3 tablespoons)

Dash of bottled hot sauce

2 cloves garlic, mashed

Combine ingredients.

Marinade for Pork

YIELDS ABOUT 2 CUPS

1½ cups dry white wine

3 tablespoons olive oil

Continued on next page

1 small onion, chopped
1 bay leaf
2 whole cloves garlic
$\frac{1}{2}$ teaspoon dried thyme
Optional: 1 small carrot, chopped; 2 allspice berries, whole; 2 juniper berries, whole

Combine ingredients.

Marionberries
See Berries

Marjoram
= oregano (smaller amounts may be required)
= thyme
= basil
= summer savory

Market mushrooms
See Mushrooms, market

Marrow beans
= great northern beans
= navy beans
= pea beans
= white beans
See Beans

Marrow squash
See Vegetable marrow

Marsala
= sweet vermouth
= Madeira
= medium sweet sherry
= port

Marshmallows
1 large = 6 miniature
11 large = 1 cup

Masa harina
See Cornmeal

Mascarpone
= cream cheese or ricotta cheese, whipped with a little butter and/or heavy cream
See Cheeses

Matsuke mushrooms
= morel mushrooms

Maui onions
See Onions, sweet

Mayonnaise, in dips

= yogurt or sour cream

Optional: Add several drops of lemon juice to taste

Melon

= papaya

= mango

Melon, crenshaw

= Spanish melon

Melon, honeydew

= Casaba melon

Melon pears, also known as pepino

See Pepino

Membrillo

= quince jelly or paste

Mesclun

See Greens

Mexican mint marigold

= tarragon

Milk, condensed

See Condensed milk (sweetened)

Milk, evaporated
= light cream or half and half
= heavy cream

Milk, in baking, up to ½ cup
= fruit juice plus ½ teaspoon baking soda added to the flour
= equal amount of fruit juice and/or water

Milk, whole, 1 cup
= 1 cup light cream (Optional: Remove up to 4 tablespoons shortening from recipe)
= ½ cup evaporated milk plus ½ cup water
= 1 cup 1 percent, 2 percent, or skim milk (Optional: Add 1 to 2 tablespoons butter or shortening)
= 3 tablespoons of milk powder plus 1 cup water (add 2 tablespoons butter or shortening if whole milk is required)
= 1 cup soy or nut milk
= 1 cup buttermilk plus ½ teaspoon baking soda

Millet
= orzo (or other tiny pasta)
= barley
= quinoa
See Grains
See Pasta

Mineola
= grapefruit and tangerine in equal amounts

Mineral water
= club soda
= seltzer

Mint
= mint or spearmint tea from tea bags or bulk tea
= crème de menthe, in sweets
= shiso
= basil

Mirin, also known as Japanese sweet rice wine
= sweet sake
= sweet sherry
= sweet vermouth

Mirliton, also known as chayote or christophine squash
See Chayote

Mizuna
= chicory or arugula
See Lettuce and salad greens

Molasses, in baking, 1 cup
= ¾ cup white or brown sugar plus ¼ cup liquid, and increase spices

Morel mushrooms
= matsuke mushrooms

Morello cherries
See Sour cherries

Moss, Irish, also known as carrageenan, 2 tablespoons
= 1 envelope or 1 tablespoon gelatin

= 2 teaspoons agar

Mulled Cider Spice Blend
YIELDS ENOUGH FOR 6 CUPS CIDER

1 cinnamon stick broken in pieces

1 whole nutmeg cut into quarters

6 whole cloves

2 teaspoons dried lemon zest

Tie up together in a piece of cheesecloth.

Mung beans
= split peas

Mushrooms
See Cêpe chanterelle, market, matsuke, morel, oyster, pied de mouton, porcini, shiitake

Mushrooms, fresh
1 lb. = 5 cups sliced

1 lb. = 12 oz. canned, drained

1 lb. = 3 oz. dried

Mushrooms, market, also known as button mushrooms

= oyster mushrooms

Mussels

= clams

= oysters

See Shellfish

Mustard, dry, 1 teaspoon

= 1 tablespoon prepared mustard from jar

Mustard, hot, Chinese

= Coleman's English dry mustard, prepared with water

Mustard, Prepared

YIELDS ½ TABLESPOON

1 teaspoon dry mustard

½ teaspoon water

2 drops vinegar

Mix well.

Mustard greens

See Lettuce and salad greens

Nam pla
= 1 part soy sauce blended with 4 parts mashed anchovies

Navy beans
= great northern beans

= marrow beans

= pea beans

= white beans

See Beans

Nectarines
= peaches

Neufchatel cheese
= cream cheese

See Cream cheese

Nigella
= black pepper (about ¼ the amount) with a pinch of
mustard seed or sesame seed

Note: Toasted = toasted sesame seed with a dash of black
pepper

Noodles
1 lb. dried = 6 to 8 cups cooked

Noodles
See Pasta

Noodles, Asian
= cellophane, also known as bean threads or vermicelli (soybean)

= lo mein

= rice stick

= soba

= udon

= vermicelli (soybean), also known as cellophane or bean threads

Note: These are made from vegetables or grains; preparation times will vary.

Nopal, also known as cactus
See Cactus

Nutmeg
= allspice

= cloves

= mace

Nuts

1 lb. shelled = 4 cups nutmeats
1 lb. in shell = 1⅔ cups nutmeats
Note: If less than ½ cup, can be
omitted from recipe.

Nuts, in baking

= bran
= soy nuts, toasted and chopped

Oats

1 cup, quick cooking = 1¾ cups cooked

Oats, in baking, 1 cup

= ¾ cup white flour

Oats, rolled, quick cooking

See Grains

Oats, rolled, regular

See Grains

Oats, steel-cut

See Grains

Octopus

= calamari, also known as squid

= squid or baby squid, also known as calamari

Oil, for cooking or frying

= canola oil, also known as rapeseed oil

= corn oil

= grapeseed oil

= light sesame oil

= olive oil

= peanut oil (adds some flavor)

= rice bran oil

= safflower oil

= soy oil

= vegetable oil

Note: The burning temperatures of different oils vary.

Oil, for baking, 1 tablespoon

= 1¼ tablespoons butter

= 1¼ tablespoons margarine

= 1 tablespoon applesauce

= 1 tablespoon mayonnaise, in cake recipes

Note: Use these substitutions only for small amounts, up to a
few tablespoons. When substituting olive or other strong
oils in baking, the baked goods may be flavored.

Oil, for salads, flavored

- = almond oil
- = Asian sesame or dark sesame oil
- = hazelnut oil
- = olive oil
- = pumpkin oil
- = walnut oil

Oil, for salads, unflavored

- = avocado oil
- = canola oil, also known as rapeseed oil
- = grapeseed oil
- = rice bran oil
- = safflower oil
- = soy oil
- = sunflower oil

Oil, for sautéing (not for deep-fat frying)

- = margarine or butter

Okra

1 medium = ¾ cup chopped

Okra

- = eggplant (texture will be different)
- = green bell peppers
- = green beans

Olallieberries

See Berries

Onion

1 medium = ½ cup chopped, fresh or frozen

Onion powder, 1 teaspoon

= 1 tablespoon minced onion

See Onion, white or yellow

Onion, white or yellow, 1 medium

= red onion, not usually used for cooking

= 1 tablespoon instant dried minced onion

= 1 tablespoon onion powder

= shallots (use up to twice the amount)

= leeks

= chives (use up to 4 times amount)

= green onions (use up to 3 times amount), also known as scallions

= scallions (use up to 3 times amount), also known as green onions

= pearl onions

Onions, green

See Green onions

Onions, sweet
Bermuda
Maui
red, also called Italian red or purple
Spanish yellow
Vidalia
Walla Walla

Orange peel, grated, up to 1 tablespoon
= tangerine peel
= marmalade
= Grand Marnier
= Curaçao
= Cointreau
= lemon or lime peel
Note: If less than 1 tablespoon, can be omitted from recipe.

Oranges
= mandarin oranges
= clementines
= satsumas
= tangerines

Oranges
1 medium = ⅓ to ½ cup juice
1 medium = 1 to 2 tablespoons
peel, finely grated

Oregano
= basil

= marjoram

= thyme

Oyster mushrooms
= button or market mushrooms

Oyster plant, also known as salsify
See Salsify

Oysters
= mussels

= clams

Note: Cooking times will vary.

See Shellfish

Pancake syrup, maple
= birch syrup

= spruce syrup

= fruit jelly, melted (add water to thin)

= dark corn syrup

Pancetta
- = bacon, cooked
- = prosciutto
- = thinly sliced ham

Panko
- = breadcrumbs, lightly toasted

Paprika, hot
- = turmeric and cayenne pepper, in equal amounts

Paprika, smoked, also known as pimentón
- = sweet paprika with a dash of smoke flavoring

Paprika, sweet
- = turmeric with a dash of red pepper

Parsley
- = chervil
- = tarragon

Parsley root
- = parsnips

Parsnips
- = parsley root
- = carrots

Passion fruit

= pomegranate mixed with much smaller amounts of apricot and grapefruit

= pomegranate

= lemon sweetened with honey, and a dash of rose or lavender flavoring, to taste

Pasta
1 8-oz. package = 5½ cups cooked

Pasta, filled

agnolotti
cannelloni
manicotti
ravioli
tortellini

Pasta, flat

egg noodles
fettuccine
linguine
tagliatelle

Pasta, medium

bucatini
Oriental (ramen) noodles
rice noodles

soba (buckwheat) noodles
spaghetti

Pasta, miscellaneous shapes
farfalle ("butterflies"; also known as bow-tie pasta)
fusilli
gnocchi (miniature potato dumplings)
pasta shells (small, medium, and large)
rotelle ("wheels")
rotini ("corkscrews")
ruote ("wagon wheels")

Pasta, thin
angel hair
capellini
fedelini
spaghettini
vermicelli

Pasta, tiny, and grain equivalents
barley
couscous
orzo
pastini
pearl couscous
rice

Pasta, tube
bocconcini

cannolicchi

ditali

macaroni

mostaccioli ("little mustaches")

penne

rigatoni

ziti

Pattypan squash, also known as summer squash

See Summer squash

Pea beans

= great northern beans

= navy beans

= marrow beans

= white beans

See Beans

Peaches
1 lb. = 4 medium
1 lb. = 2 cups, sliced, peeled

Peaches

= nectarines

= cantaloupe

Peanut butter, up to ¼ cup

= sesame paste

= almond or other nut butters

Note: Add 1 teaspoon oil or other liquid if substitutes are stiff.

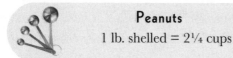

Peanuts
1 lb. shelled = 2¼ cups

Pear-apples
See Pears

Pearl couscous, also known as Israeli couscous
See Couscous

Pearl onions
See Onions

Pearl onions
1 small onion = 4 pearl onions

Pears
= Asian pears

= apples

Peas
1 lb. in pod = 1 cup shelled

Pecans
1 lb. shelled = 3 to 4 cups nutmeats

Pecans
= walnuts, in small amounts

Pepino, also known as melon pears
= pears with a dash of vanilla
= melon

Pepper
See Black pepper, cayenne pepper, chili pepper, hot red pepper, pink pepper, red pepper

Pepper, aleppo
= crushed red pepper flakes

Pepper, Lemon
YIELDS ABOUT ⅓ CUP
3 tablespoons freshly ground pepper
3 tablespoons lemon zest
1 tablespoon chopped chives

Peppercorns
= black peppercorns
= green peppercorns
= pink peppercorns
= white peppercorns
Note: Peppercorns vary in strength.

Pepperoni
- = sausage, cooked
- = salami

Peppers
1 cup uncooked = ½ cup cooked
1 lb. = 2 to 2½ cups uncooked
1 large = ¾ to 1 cup chopped

Peppers, chili
- = cayenne
- = fresno
- = habanero
- = jalapeno
- = pequin
- = Scotch bonnet
- = serrano
- = Thai

Note: Chili Peppers vary greatly in strength from mild to extra hot, so use care when attempting substitutions.

Peppers, chili, milder
- = Anaheim
- = ancho (dried poblano)
- = banana peppers
- = cherry peppers
- = chile verde, green

= chile Colorado, red

= Hungarian wax

= pasilla, also known as poblano

= pepperoncini

= poblano, also known as pasilla (called ancho when dried)

= Tuscan

Peppers, gold

See Peppers, yellow

Peppers, green or bell

= Anaheim

= celery

= jicama

= orange peppers

= pimiento

= red peppers

= sweet banana peppers

= water chestnuts

= yellow peppers

Peppers, red sweet

= green peppers

= orange peppers

= yellow peppers

Note: These are bell peppers, not chile peppers.

Peppers, yellow, also known as gold peppers
= green peppers
= orange peppers
= red peppers
Note: These are bell peppers, not chile peppers.

Pepper Shake, Spicy
YIELDS ABOUT ½ CUP

1 tablespoon cayenne pepper

2 tablespoons garlic powder

2 tablespoons paprika

2 tablespoons parsley

2 tablespoons ground black pepper

½ tablespoon salt (optional)

Persimmon
= pureed cooked squash or pumpkin, sweetened
= mashed banana mixed with equal amount of drained, crushed pineapple
= mango

Pesto
YIELDS 2 CUPS

2 cups fresh basil leaves, washed and thoroughly dried

2 cloves garlic

Continued on next page

$\frac{1}{2}$ cup olive oil

1 cup freshly grated Parmesan or Pecorino Romano cheese

$\frac{1}{2}$ cup toasted pine nuts or shelled, toasted walnuts

Process in a blender or food processor until smooth. Serve at room temperature.

Petit pois
= baby green peas

= pigeon peas

= gunga peas

Pickle relish, sweet
= chopped sweet pickles

Pickling Spice
YIELDS ABOUT 1 CUP

4 3-inch cinnamon sticks

1 1-inch piece dried ginger

2 tablespoons mustard seed

2 teaspoons whole allspice

2 teaspoons black peppercorns

2 teaspoons whole cloves

2 teaspoons dill seed

2 teaspoons coriander seed

2 teaspoons ground mace

Continued on next page

8 bay leaves, crumbled
Optional: 1 to 1½-inch dried red chile pepper, chopped

Combine ingredients.

Pied de mouton, also known as hedgehog mushrooms
= chanterelles

Pie Spice, Pumpkin or Apple
YIELDS ENOUGH FOR ONE 9-INCH PIE

½ teaspoon cinnamon
¼ teaspoon nutmeg
¼ teaspoon ground cloves
⅛ teaspoon allspice
⅛ teaspoon cardamom

Combine spices.

Pigeon peas, also known as gunga peas
= lentils
= chickpeas

Pignoli, also known as pine nuts
See Pine nuts

Pimento
= sweet red peppers, roasted and peeled

Pimentón

See Paprika, smoked

Pineapple guava, also known as feijoa

= pineapple flavored with a little strawberry and banana

= pineapple and grapes and a dash of lemon, and mint

Pine nuts, also known as pignoli

= chopped walnuts

= blanched, peeled, slivered almonds

Pink beans

= pinto beans

= red beans

= kidney beans

Pink peppercorns

= black peppercorns

Pinto beans

= pink beans

= red beans

= kidney beans

Pita bread

= flour tortillas

Plantains, also known as platanos

= bananas

= sweet potatoes

= parsnips

Note: Use cooked parsnips only.

See Boniato

Platanos, also known as plantains

See Plantains

Plums

= pluots

= fresh figs

Note: Greengage, damson, and Italian/black have distinct
flavors.

Plum Sauce, also known as Duck Sauce
YIELDS ABOUT ¼ CUP
¼ cup apricot jelly or plum jelly
1 teaspoon vinegar
1½ teaspoons sugar
Stir together until sugar dissolves.

Pluots

= plums

= apricots

= fresh figs

Polenta
= cornmeal
= grits

Pomegranate juice
= grenadine with a dash of lemon juice

Pomelo, also known as pummelo
= grapefruit

Ponzu Sauce

YIELDS ABOUT 3 TABLESPOONS

2 tablespoons soy sauce

1 tablespoon lemon juice

Combine.

Porcini mushrooms, also known as cêpe or boletus mushrooms
= shiitake mushrooms

Pork, ground
= sausage meat (omit salt and other spices from recipe)

Pork fat, fresh
= salt pork, boiled briefly (omit salt from recipe)
= unsmoked bacon, boiled briefly (omit salt from recipe)

Port

= Madeira

= sherry

= Marsala

Potatoes

1 lb. = 3 medium

1 lb. = 3 cups sliced

1 lb. = 2¼ cups cooked

1 lb. = 1¾ cups mashed

Poultry Seasoning

YIELDS ABOUT ½ CUP

2 tablespoons dried marjoram

2 tablespoons dried savory

2 teaspoons dried parsley

1 tablespoon dried sage

1½ teaspoons dried thyme

Combine.

Powdered sugar

See Sugar, powdered

Prawns

= shrimp

= crayfish

= langouste

= langoustine

= lobster

See Shellfish

Prosciutto

= smoked ham

= country ham

= bacon, cooked

Prunes
1 lb. = 2¼ cups pitted

Prunes

= dates

= raisins

= dried apricots

Note: If less than ¼ cup, can be omitted from recipe.

Pulses

See individual pulses such as beans, lentils, or peas

Pummelo, also known as pomelo

See Pomelo

Pumpkin

See Squash, winter

Puntarella
= chicory, Italian

Quail
= Cornish game hen

= squab

Quatre epices, 1 teaspoon
=1 teaspoon allspice

Quatre Epices
YIELDS 1 TEASPOON

¼ teaspoon black pepper

¼ teaspoon nutmeg

¼ teaspoon ginger

¼ teaspoon cloves

Mix together.

Quince
= sour cherries

= cranberries

= tart cooking apples

Quince, paste or jelly
= membrillo

Quinoa
= couscous
= millet
See Rice, grains

Rabbit
= chicken

Radicchio
See Lettuce and salad greens

Radish
= daikon radish
= grated horseradish
= jicama (for texture)

Rainier cherries
See Cherries, red

Raisins

= currant, dried

= golden raisins

= soft prunes or dates, finely chopped

= sultanas

Note: If less than ½ cup, can be omitted from recipe.

Raisins, golden

See Raisins

Ramps

= leeks

= green onions, also known as scallions

Rapini, also known as broccoli rabe

See Greens

Raspberries

= blackberries

= boysenberries

See Berries

Red beans

= pinto beans

= pink beans

= kidney beans

Red cabbage

= green cabbage

Red kuri squash

See Squash, winter

Red onions

= Bermuda onions

= Maui onions

= Vidalia onions

See Onions, sweet

Red pepper, ground

= cayenne pepper

= chili powder

= hot pepper sauce

= bottled hot sauce

= hot red pepper flakes

Red pepper flakes, hot

= chopped, dried red chile peppers

= powdered red chile pepper (different amounts may be required)

Red pepper oil, also known as chile oil

See Chile oil

Red pepper sauce, hot

See Hot pepper sauce

Red peppers, sweet

See Peppers

Red wine vinegar

See Vinegar

Rice

1 cup uncooked = 3 cups cooked
1 lb. = 2 to 2½ cups uncooked

Rice

Grains may be served instead of rice, or rice can be substituted for them in recipes.

= arborio rice

= basmati rice

= black Japonica rice

= Chinese black rice, also known as Chinese forbidden black rice

= Colusari red rice

= Himalayan red rice

= jasmine rice

= purple Thai rice

= short- and medium-grain white rice

= short- and medium-grain brown rice

= spelt

= quinoa

= wild rice

See Grains

Rice sticks

See Noodles, Asian

Rice Vinegar, Seasoned, also known as Sweet Rice Vinegar

YIELDS ABOUT ¼ CUP

3 tablespoons white wine vinegar

1 tablespoon sugar

Combine.

Rice wine
See Sake

Rice wine, sweet Japanese, also known as mirin
See Mirin

Risotto, also known as arborio rice
= short-grain white rice
= short-grain brown rice

Rocket, also known as arugula
See Arugula

Romaine
See Lettuce and salad greens

Rosemary
= marjoram
= thyme

Rum

= brandy

= cognac

Rutabaga, also known as swede

= turnip

Rye berries

See Grains

Saffron, also known as azafran

= safflower (larger amounts may be required)

For color

= achiote, also known as annatto

= turmeric

= marigold petals, dried

Sage

= poultry seasoning

= savory

= marjoram

= rosemary

= oregano

Sake

= dry sherry or vermouth

= Chinese rice wine

Salami

= pepperoni

Salmonberries

See Berries

Salsa
YIELDS ABOUT 2 CUPS
4 tomatoes, fresh or canned, chopped
½ cup green or red onions, chopped
¼ cup cilantro, chopped
2 cloves garlic, minced
½ teaspoon salt
1 small jalapeno pepper, seeded and chopped
2 tablespoons lime juice or red wine vinegar
1 teaspoon olive oil
Combine all ingredients.

Salsify, also known as oyster plant

= parsnip (needs a longer cooking time)

Salt, coarse

= kosher salt

Salt, for savory dishes, up to 1 teaspoon

= soy sauce, to taste

Salt, kosher

= coarse salt

Salt, sea

= fleur de sel

Salt, Seasoned I

YIELDS ABOUT 1¼ CUP

1 cup salt

2½ teaspoons paprika

2 teaspoons dry mustard

1½ teaspoons oregano

1 teaspoon garlic powder

1 teaspoon onion powder

Mix until well blended.

Salt, Seasoned II

YIELDS ABOUT ⅔ CUP

½ cup salt

2 teaspoons ground pepper, black or white

2 teaspoons celery seeds

Continued on next page

2 teaspoons cumin

2 teaspoons paprika

Pinch sugar (optional)

For spicy seasoned salt, add 1 teaspoon cayenne pepper

Mix together until well blended.

Salt substitute (as a flavor enhancer)

= black pepper

= garlic

= onion powder

= mustard powder

= paprika

= red pepper

= lemon juice

= vinegar

= wine (not cooking wine)

Salt Substitute I

YIELDS ABOUT ¼ CUP

1 tablespoon garlic powder

1 tablespoon powdered or crushed dried basil

1 tablespoon powdered or crushed dried oregano

½ tablespoon finely minced, dried lemon zest

Mix together until well blended.

Salt Substitute II

YIELDS ½ CUP

1 tablespoon ground pepper

1 tablespoon celery seed

1 tablespoon ground coriander

2 tablespoons paprika

3 tablespoons crushed, dried summer savory

Mix together until well blended.

Sambal

YIELDS ABOUT 1 CUP

2 cloves garlic

½ cup dried hot red chilies, seeded

1 onion sliced

4 tablespoons sugar

4 tablespoons lemon juice

4 tablespoons water

Blend ingredients in a food processor and then simmer for 10 minutes. Let cool before serving.

Sapote

= mango with a little vanilla custard or a dash of vanilla, to taste

= a mixture of peaches and vanilla custard flavored with lemon, to taste

Sardines, processed
= small herring
= small mackerel

Sassafras, also known as filé powder or gumbo filé
= cumin with ¼ amount cornstarch for thickening

Satsumas
= tangerines
= clementines
= mandarin oranges
= oranges

Sausage
= pepperoni
= ground pork with sage, marjoram, garlic, and onions to taste

Savory, summer
= thyme and half the amount of mint
= sage

Savory, winter
= pepper and ¼ the amount of bay leaf

Savoy cabbage
- = Chinese cabbage
- = kohlrabi
- = lettuce
- = Brussels sprouts, shredded (in cooked dishes)

Scallions, also known as green onions
See Green onions

Scallops
- = shark

Seasoned rice vinegar, also known as sweet rice vinegar
See Rice vinegar

Seltzer
See Club soda

Semolina
- = farina
- = cream of wheat

Sesame seed
- = finely chopped almonds

Shallots
- = green onions, also known as scallions

= leeks

= onions (use ⅔ amount)

See Onions, green

Shellfish

Note: Some shellfish can be substituted for each other; preparation and cooking times will vary.

See Abalone, cockles, clams, crab, crayfish, langouste, langoustine, lobster, mussels, oysters, prawns, shrimp

Sherry

= Madeira

= port

= Marsala

Sherry vinegar

See Vinegar

Shiitake mushrooms

= boletus mushrooms, also known as cèpe or porcini mushrooms

= cèpe mushrooms, also known as boletus or porcini mushrooms

= porcini mushrooms, also known as boletus or cèpe mushrooms

= meat, especially tender steak or veal

Shiso
= basil

= mint

Shortening, in baking
= butter

= margarine

See Butter, in baking

Shrimp
= prawns

= crayfish

= langouste

= langoustine

See Shellfish

Snails
= shrimp

Snow peas
= sugar snap peas

Soba noodles
See Noodles, Asian

Softshell crab
See Crab

Sorrel

= spinach (add a few drops of lemon)

See Greens

See Lettuce and salad greens

Sour cherries

= cranberries

= gooseberries

= currants, fresh

= quince

Note: These fruits are usually cooked.

Sour cream, 1 cup

= 1 tablespoon white vinegar plus enough milk to make 1 cup (let stand 5 minutes before using)

= 1 tablespoon lemon juice plus enough evaporated milk to make 1 cup (let stand 5 minutes before using)

= 1 cup plain yogurt, especially in dips and cold soups

= ⅞ cup cottage cheese blended to break up curds (mixed with yogurt if desired) and 2 tablespoons milk and 1 tablespoon lemon juice; blend well

= 6 ounces cream cheese plus 3 tablespoons milk

= ⅓ cup melted butter plus ¾ cup sour milk, for baking

Sour milk, 1 cup

= 1½ tablespoons lemon juice or vinegar plus enough milk to make 1 cup

Note: With pasteurized milk, this is the only way to make

sour milk. Pasteurized milk will spoil, but it will not go sour like raw milk.

Soursop, also known as guanabana
= cherimoya
= custard apple
= sweetsop
= melons and peaches
= guavas and peaches

Soy beans, also known as edamame
= lima beans
= broad beans
= fava beans

Soy milk
= milk

Soy Sauce
YIELDS ¼ CUP
3 tablespoons Worcestershire sauce
1 tablespoon water
¼ teaspoon salt
Combine.
Note: Light and dark soy sauce can be substituted for each other.

Soy Sauce, Indonesian-Style

YIELDS ABOUT 1 CUP

½ cup soy sauce

¼ cup dark brown sugar

3 tablespoons dark corn syrup

1 tablespoon molasses

Combine.

Spaghetti
1 lb. = about 6 cups cooked

Spaghetti

= spaghetti squash

See Pasta

Spaghetti squash

See Squash, winter

Spelt

= barley

= farro

= wheat berries

See Grains

Spinach
1 lb. fresh = ½ cup cooked

Spinach

See Greens

Spiny lobster

= crayfish

= langouste

= langoustine

= lobster

= prawns

= shrimp

See Shellfish

Split peas

= mung beans, in salads

= lentils, in soups or stews

Sprouts

The following sprouts are interchangeable:

alfalfa

bean

buckwheat

sunflower

Note: Radish sprouts are spicier.

Squab

= Cornish game hen

= chicken

= grouse

= pigeon

= quail

Squash, summer

chayote, also known as mirliton or christophine

courgettes, also known as zucchini

pattypan, also known as white squash

vegetable marrow

white squash, also known as pattypan

yellow squash (straight or crooked neck)

zucchini, also known as courgettes

Squash, winter

acorn

amber cup

Australian blue

autumn cup

banana

buttercup

butternut

calabazo, also known as West Indian pumpkin or Cuban squash

carnival

Cuban squash, also known as calabazo or West Indian Pumpkin

delicata

golden nugget
hubbard
kabocha
pumpkin
red kuri squash
spaghetti squash
sweet dumpling squash
table queen
turban
West Indian pumpkin, also known as calabazo or Cuban squash

Squid, also known as calamari

= octopus or baby octopus

Star anise, also known as anise seed

= fennel seed
See Anise seed

Starfruit, also known as carambola

= watermelon with a few dashes of lemon juice

Stock—chicken, beef, veal, fish, vegetable

= bouillon
= consommé
Note: Stock in a sauce may be replaced by wine for up to ⅓ of stock required.

Stone crab
See Crab

> ### Sugar
> granulated white, 1 lb. = 2 cups
> granulated white, 1 cup = 6¾ ounces,
> approximately
> powdered or confectioners, 1 lb. = 3½ cups
> frmly packed brown, 1 lb. = 2¼ cups

Sugar, brown, ½ cup
= ½ cup white sugar plus 2 tablespoons molasses

Note: To replace a combination of brown sugar and milk, use honey or molasses with powdered milk.

Sugar, caster
See Sugar, superfine

Sugar, granulated white, 1 cup
= 1 cup superfine sugar

= 1 cup turbinado sugar

= 1 cup firmly packed brown sugar

= 2 cups powdered sugar, sifted

= ¾ cup honey or 1¼ cups molasses and reduce other liquid in recipe by ¼ cup; or add ¼ cup flour if no other liquid is called for

= 1 cup corn syrup, but never replace more than half the amount of sugar this way; and reduce other liquid in the recipe by ¼ cup for each 2 cups sugar substituted this way

Note:
- Sugar generally may be reduced by a quarter of the amount.
- Sugar can be reduced by ½ cup if liquid is reduced by ¼ cup.
- A few tablespoons of granulated sugar may be replaced by maple sugar.
- Consult manufacturers of artificial sweeteners for recipes using those products.

Sugar, icing
See Sugar, powdered

Sugar, powdered, 1 cup sifted
= ½ cup granulated white sugar
Note: Granulated sugar takes longer to dissolve.

Sugar, superfine
= granulated sugar
Note: Granulated sugar takes longer to dissolve.

Sugar, Vanilla
YIELDS 2 CUPS

2 cups sugar

Continued on next page

2 vanilla beans

Cover vanilla beans with sugar. Store in an airtight container for at least 24 hours. Replenish sugar as used until vanilla aromas are depleted.

Sugar snap peas

= snow peas

Sultanas

= currants, dried

= golden raisins

= soft prunes or dates, finely chopped

= raisins

Note: If less than $\frac{1}{2}$ cup, can be omitted from recipe.

Sumac

= lemongrass

= lemon verbena

= zaatar

Summer savory

See Savory, summer

Summer squash

See Squash, summer

Sunchokes, also known as Jerusalem artichokes
See Jerusalem artichokes

Sunflower sprouts
= watercress
See Sprouts

Swede
See Rutabaga

Sweet dumpling squash
See Squash, winter

Sweet onion
See Onions, sweet

Sweet potatoes
= yams
See Boniato

Sweet rice vinegar, also known as seasoned rice vinegar
See Rice vinegar

Sweetsop
= cherimoya
= atemoya
See Soursop

Swiss chard

See Greens

Table queen squash

See Squash, winter

Tahini

= ground sesame seeds, finely ground and made into a paste with olive or sesame oil

= unsalted sunflower seeds or blanched almonds, finely ground into a paste with vegetable oil

Tamarind

= dried apricots and dates with lemon juice to taste

= chopped prunes, with lemon juice

Tamarind paste

= dried apricots and dates with lemon juice to taste

= chopped prunes, with lemon juice

Tamarind pods

= lemon juice

Tangerines

- = satsumas
- = mandarin oranges
- = clementines
- = oranges

Taro, also known as dasheen

- = sweet potato
- = yam
- = parsnip

See Dasheen

Tarragon

- = anise (use ¹/₂ amount)
- = Mexican mint marigold (larger amount may be required)
- = chervil (use 1¹/₂ times amount)

Tartar Sauce
YIELDS ABOUT ½ CUP
2 tablespoons sweet pickle relish or sweet pickles, chopped
4 tablespoons mayonnaise
1 tablespoon onion, chopped (optional)
1 tablespoon hard-boiled egg, chopped (optional)
a few drops lemon juice (optional)
¹/₂ teaspoon mustard (optional)

Continued on next page

¹/₂ teaspoon dill (optional)

Combine.

Tea
1 lb. leaves = 100 servings

Teriyaki Sauce
YIELDS ½ CUP

5 tablespoons soy sauce
3 tablespoons seasoned rice vinegar
1 teaspoon ginger, powdered or fresh, minced

Combine and mix well.

Thousand Island Dressing
YIELDS ABOUT 1¾ CUPS

1 cup mayonnaise
¹/₄ cup chili sauce
¹/₄ cup ketchup
¹/₄ cup pickle relish
1 chopped hard-boiled egg

Combine and stir well.

Thyme
- = marjoram
- = oregano
- = summer savory
- = bay leaf (remove before serving)

Tomatillos
- = fresh green tomatoes with a few dashes of lemon juice
- = green tomatoes
- = ground cherries

Tomatoes, canned, 1 cup
- = 1⅓ cups chopped fresh tomatoes, simmered

Tomatoes, cooked, seasoned, 1 lb.
- = 8 ounces tomato sauce, for cooking

Tomatoes, fresh
1 lb. = 2 to 3 medium
1 lb. = 8 ounces canned
1 lb. = 1½ cups chopped

Tomato juice, 1 cup
- = 2 or 3 fresh, ripe tomatoes, peeled, seeded, and blended in blender or food processor (add salt and lemon juice to taste)
- = ½ cup tomato sauce plus ½ cup water for cooking

Tomato paste, 1 tablespoon

= 1 tablespoon ketchup

= ¼ cup tomato sauce (and boil longer or reduce some other liquid from recipe)

Tomato puree, 1 cup

= 1 cup tomato sauce

= ½ cup tomato paste plus ½ cup water

Tomato sauce, 2 cups

= ¾ cup tomato paste plus 1 cup water

= 2 cups tomato puree

Tortillas

= pita bread, split open

= lavash bread

Triticale, flaked

= rolled oats

Triticale berries

= wheat berries

Truffles, fresh

= canned truffles or canned truffle peels; add canning liquid if possible

= truffle oil for flavoring

Note: Fresh truffles are much more aromatic.

Tuna, canned
= albacore
= cooked, boned chicken

Tunisian hot sauce
See Harissa

Turban squash
See Squash, winter

Turkey
= chicken

Turmeric
= mustard powder, with an optional dash of saffron

Turnip greens
See Greens

Turnips, for cooking
= rutabaga
= swede
= kohlrabi

Turnips, raw
= jicama
= radish

Tuscan kale
See Kale, Tuscan

Twentieth century pears
See Asian pears

Udon noodles
See Noodles, Asian

Ugli or ugli fruit
= grapefruit sweetened with sugar to taste

Vanilla extract, in baking
= Tuaca liqueur
= almond, peppermint, or other extracts (smaller amounts may be required)

Note: These will alter the flavor of the finished product.

Veal, scallops
= boned, skinned chicken breasts
= turkey breast slices

Vegetable marrow
= zucchini, also known as courgettes
See Squash, summer

Verbena
= lemon peel
= lemongrass
= sumac

Vermicelli
See Pasta

Vermicelli (soybean), also known as bean thread and cellophane noodles
See Noodles, Asian

Vidalia onions
See Onions, sweet

Vienna sausages
= frankfurters, sliced
= hot dogs, sliced
= knockwurst, sliced

Vinegar
   = lemon juice, in cooking and salads
   = grapefruit juice, in salads
   = wine, in marinades

Vinegar, medium
   apple cider vinegar
   champagne vinegar
   flavored vinegars
   malt vinegar
   red wine vinegar
   rice vinegar
   rice vinegar, sweet
   sherry vinegar
   white vinegar
   white wine vinegar

Vinegar, strong
   balsamic vinegar
   white balsamic vinegar

Walla Walla onions
   See Onions, sweet

Wasabi, powdered
= horseradish
= mustard
= daikon radish

Wasabi, prepared, 1 tablespoon
= 1 tablespoon hot dry mustard plus 1½ teaspoons vinegar

Water chestnuts
= jicama, raw

Watercress
= sunflower sprouts
See Lettuce and salad greens
See Greens

Wax beans
= green beans

West Indian pumpkin, also known as calabazo or Cuban squash
See Squash, winter

Wheat, cracked
See Grains

Wheat berries
= farro

= barley
= spelt
See Grains

Whiskey

= bourbon

White balsamic vinegar

See Vinegar

White beans

= great northern beans
= pea beans
= marrow beans
= navy beans
See Beans

White peppercorns

= black peppercorns
= pink peppercorns
Note: Peppercorns vary in strength.

White sweet potatoes

See Boniato

White vinegar

See Vinegar

White wine vinegar
See Vinegar

Wild rice
See Rice
See Grains

Wine, for marinades, ½ cup
= ¼ cup vinegar plus 1 tablespoon sugar plus 3 tablespoons water

Winter melon
= zucchini
= fuzzy melon
= chayote

Winter savory
See Savory, winter

Winter squash
See Squash, winter

Wood ear mushrooms
= cloud ear mushrooms
= black fungus mushrooms
= silver ear mushrooms

Worcestershire Sauce

MAKES ABOUT 2 TEASPOONS

1 teaspoon soy sauce or vinegar

¼ teaspoon tamarind paste or sugar or molasses

¼ teaspoon anchovy paste

⅛ teaspoon onion powder or minced onions, crushed

2 drops hot pepper sauce

1 dash nutmeg or mace

Optional: 1 dash lemon juice

Mix well.

Yams

= sweet potatoes

See Boniato

Yeast, compressed, 1 cake

= 2 envelopes dry yeast

= 2 tablespoons powdered yeast

Yeast, dry, 1 envelope

= 1 tablespoon powdered yeast

= ½ cake compressed yeast, crumbled

Yellow finn potatoes

= yukon gold potatoes

Yellow onions

See Onions

Yellow peppers, also known as gold peppers

See Peppers

Yellow squash, crookneck or straightneck

= pattypan squash

= zucchini

See Squash, summer

Yogurt, plain

= sour cream

= crème fraîche

= buttermilk

= heavy cream

= cottage cheese and half the amount of mayonnaise blended smooth (only up to ¼ cup, for salads or dips)

Youngberries

See Berries

Yuca, also known as manioc or cassava

See Cassava

Yukon gold potatoes

    = yellow finn potatoes

    = potatoes

Yuzu

    = lemon juice and grapefruit juice in equal amounts

Zaatar
YIELDS 1 TABLESPOON
1 teaspoon sumac
1 teaspoon summer savory
1 teaspoon roasted sesame seed
¼ teaspoon salt
Optional: Add ½ teaspoon cumin and/or oregano
Grind together with mortar and pestle.

Zucchini, also known as courgettes

    = pattypan squash

    = yellow crookneck squash

    = yellow straightneck squash

    See Squash, summer

Herbs and Spices at a Glance

Herb/Spice	Substitute
achiote	turmeric; saffron
allspice	ground cloves with cinnamon and nutmeg to taste, in baking; black pepper, in cooking
anise	fennel; tarragon; chervil (use up to twice the amount)
anise, green	fennel seed
anise seed, also known as star anise	fennel seed; caraway seed (use 1½ times the amount); chervil (use twice the amount)
asafetida	equal parts onion powder, celery seed, curry powder, and cumin
basil, dried	oregano; parsley; summer savory
basil, lemon	basil

Herb/Spice	Substitute
basil, mint	shiso
bergamot	orange flavoring with a dash of lavender, to taste
black pepper	white pepper; allspice in cooking
caraway seed	fennel seed; cumin seed
cardamom	cinnamon; mace
cassia	cinnamon, mace
cayenne pepper	ground hot red pepper; chili powder
celery seed	dill seed
chervil	tarragon (use $\frac{1}{2}$ the amount); anise (use $\frac{1}{2}$ the amount); Italian parsley
Chinese parsley	see cilantro
chives	green onion tops; onion powder (use small amount); leeks; shallots (use less)
cilantro, also known as coriander leaf, Chinese parsley	parsley with a dash of lemon juice; orange peel with a pinch of sage; lemon grass with a pinch of mint; parsley and mint in equal amounts; Italian parsley (for garnish)

Herb/Spice	Substitute
cinnamon	cardamom with ⅛ the amount allspice or nutmeg; ¼ the amount allspice; ¼ the amount nutmeg
cloves, ground	allspice; nutmeg; mace
coarse salt	kosher salt; sea salt
coriander leaf	see cilantro
coriander seed	caraway with a dash of cumin; lemon flavoring with a dash of sage; allspice with a pinch of lemon or lemon zest
cumin	caraway and anise; fennel seed
dill seed	caraway seed; celery seed
fennel seed	caraway seed; anise, also known as anise seed; star anise
fenugreek	celery seed; lovage
filé powder	see gumbo filé
fleur de sel	sea salt
galangal (Laos powder)	ginger root; powdered ginger with a dash of cardamom

Herb/Spice	Substitute
ginger, fresh, grated	powdered ginger (about ¼ the amount) with a dash of white pepper and lemon juice; minced, crystallized ginger with sugar washed off
ginger, powdered	grated fresh ginger, mace with a pinch of lemon peel; nutmeg (about ¼ the amount)
gumbo filé, also known as filé powder	sassafras
horseradish, fresh, grated	daikon radish; wasabi
hot red pepper flakes	chopped, dried red chile peppers; powdered red chile pepper (use less)
kosher salt	coarse salt
mace	allspice; cloves; nutmeg (optional: add dash of cardamom)
marjoram	oregano (a smaller amount may be required); thyme, basil; summer savory
Mexican mint marigold	tarragon

Herb/Spice	Substitute
mint	mint or spearmint tea from tea bags or bulk tea; crème de menthe, in sweets; shiso; basil
nigella	black pepper (about ¼ the amount) with a dash of mustard seed or sesame seed; toasted nigella = toasted sesame seed with a dash of black pepper
nutmeg	allspice; cloves; mace
oregano	marjoram; thyme; basil
paprika, hot	turmeric and cayenne pepper, in equal amounts
paprika, smoked, also known as pimentón	sweet paprika with a dash of smoke flavoring
paprika, sweet	turmeric with a dash of red pepper
parsley	chervil; tarragon
pepper, aleppo	crushed red pepper flakes
red pepper, ground	cayenne pepper; chili powder; hot pepper sauce; bottled hot sauce; hot red pepper flakes
rosemary	marjoram; thyme

Herb/Spice	Substitute
saffron	turmeric; achiote, also known as annatto
sage	poultry seasoning; marjoram; savory; rosemary
salt substitutes (flavor enhancers)	black pepper; garlic; onion powder; mustard powder; paprika; red pepper; lemon juice; vinegar; wine (not cooking wines)
sesame seed	finely chopped almonds
shiso	basil; mint
sumac	lemongrass; lemon verbena; zaatar
summer savory	thyme and ½ the amount of mint, sage
tarragon	anise (use ½ the amount); Mexican mint marigold (larger amount may be required); chervil (use 1½ times the amount)
thyme	marjoram; oregano; winter savory; bay leaf
turmeric	mustard powder (optional: add saffron)
wasabi, powdered	horseradish; mustard; daikon radish
winter savory	pepper and ¼ the amount of bay leaf

Measurement Equivalents

Here is a list of commonly used measuring equivalents for cooking and baking. Some amounts have been rounded for convenience.

FOOD MEASURING EQUIVALENTS

Dry Measurements

1 pinch = ⅛ teaspoon, approximately
½ tablespoon = 1½ teaspoons
3 teaspoons = 1 tablespoon
¼ cup = 4 tablespoons
⅓ cup = 5 tablespoons plus 1 teaspoon
⅜ cup = 6 tablespoons
½ cup = 8 tablespoons
⅔ cup = 10 tablespoons plus 2 teaspoons
¾ cup = 12 tablespoons
1 cup = 16 tablespoons

4 cups = 1 quart

8 quarts = 1 peck*

4 pecks = 1 bushel*

* for large fruits and vegetables, not berries

Liquid Measurements

1 dash = a few drops

1 tablespoon = 3 teaspoons

1 tablespoon = ½ fluid ounce

1 fluid ounce = 2 tablespoons

1 jigger = 3 tablespoons or 1½ fluid ounces

¼ cup = 4 tablespoons or 2 fluid ounces

1 cup = 8 tablespoons or 4 fluid ounces

1 cup = 16 tablespoons or 8 fluid ounces

1 pint (U.S.) = 2 cups or 16 fluid ounces

1 pint (Imperial) = 19 fluid ounces (20 Imperial fluid ounces)

1 quart (U.S.) = 2 pints or 32 fluid ounces

1 gallon (U.S.) = 4 quarts or 132 U.S. fluid ounces

1 gallon (Imperial) = 154 fluid ounces (160 Imperial fluid ounces)

Fluid Ounces	=	Milliliters
1		30
2		60
4		120
6		180
8 (1 cup)		235
16 (1 U.S. pint)		475
20 (1 imperial pint)		568
32 (1 quart)		945

Note: 1 quart = .946 liter
1 liter = 1.057 quarts

METRIC EQUIVALENTS

Ounces = Grams	
1	28
2	57
3	85
4	113
5	142
6	170
7	198
8	227
9	255
10	284
11	312
12	340
13	368
14	397
15	425
16	454

Grams = Ounces	
1	.035
50	1.75
100	3.5
250	8.75
500	17.5
750	26.25
100 (1 kilogram)	35 (2.21 lbs.)

Pounds = Kilograms	
1	.45
2	.91
3	1.4
4	1.8
5	2.3
6	2.7
7	3.2
8	3.5
9	4.1
10	4.5

Kilograms = Pounds	
1	2.2
2	4.4
3	6.6
4	8.8
5	11

TEMPERATURE EQUIVALENTS

Temperature	Degrees Fahrenheit	Degrees Celcius (Centigrade)	Gas Mark
Room temperature	70	21	1,275 or slow
Lukewarm	90	32	2,300 or slow
Water's boiling point	212	100	3,325 or moderate
Low or cool oven	250	121	4,350 or moderate
Slow oven	300	149	5,375 or moderately hot
Moderately slow oven	325	163	6,400 or moderately hot
Moderate oven	350	177	7,425 or hot
Moderately hot oven	375	190	8,450 or hot
Hot oven	400	204	9,475 or very hot
Very hot oven	450 to 500	232 to 260	
Broil	550	288	

BAKING PAN SIZES

Note: Adjust baking times when changing pan sizes.

Cake pans, rectangular

8″ x 8″ x 2″
- = 6 cups
- = 20 cm x 20 cm x 5 cm

9″ x 9″ x 1½″
- = 6 cups
- = 23 cm x 23 cm x 4 cm

9″ x 9″ x 2″
- = 7 cups
- = 23 cm x 23 cm x 5 cm

13″ x 9″ x 2″
- = 10 cups
- = 33 cm x 23 cm x 5 cm

Cake pans, round

8″ x 1½″
- = 4 cups
- = 20 cm x 4 cm

9″ x 1½″
- = 6 cups
- = 23 cm x 4 cm

Loaf pans

8½″ x 4½″ x 2½″
- = 6 cups
- = 22 cm x 11 cm x 6 cm

9″ x 5″ x 3″
- = 8 cups
- = 23 cm x 13 cm x 8 cm

Pie pans

8″ x 1¼″
- = 3 cups, level
- = 4½ cups, mounded
- = 20 cm x 3 cm

9″ x 1½″
- = 4 cups, level
- = 5 to 6 cups, mounded
- = 23 cm x 4 cm

Springform pans

8″ x 3″
- = 10 cups
- = 20 cm x 8 cm

9″ x 3″

   = 11 cups

   = 23 cm x 9 cm

10″ x 3¾″

   = 12 cups

   = 25 cm x 10 cm

Tube pans or ring molds

8½″ x 2¼″

   = 4½ cups

   = 22 cm x 6 cm

7½″ x 3″

   = 6 cups

   = 19 cm x 8 cm

9¼″ x 2¾″

   = 8 cups

   = 23 cm x 7 cm

Too Much, Too Little, Too Late: Remedies for Common Kitchen Disasters

Here is a collection of simple fixes to try for many of life's little disasters in the kitchen.

Alcohol
If too much is poured into punch or other mixed alcoholic drinks, float thin slices of cucumber to absorb the alcohol taste.

Baking powder
To test for viability, put a teaspoon into a cup of hot water. It will bubble if the baking powder is still fresh.

Beans are overcooked
Add a little vinegar or lemon juice.

Beans are too tough
First add a teaspoon of baking soda to cooking water. Salt cooking water lightly. Do not add acidic ingredients like tomatoes until after beans are cooked.

Bread is overcooked

Poke holes with a knife or skewer and drizzle sparingly with fruit juice, milk, or honey while bread is warm.

Bread is undercooked

Cover with aluminum foil and return to oven for a few minutes at a time, until done.

Butter burned during frying

To prevent butter from browning, substitute oil for half the butter.

Coffee is too bitter (from overheating)

Add a pinch of salt to the cup.

It's best to turn off the coffee pot after no more than 14 minutes. Later, the cooled coffee will taste fresh when reheated to drinking temperature in microwave.

Corn is bland

Add several spoonfuls of sugar to the cooking water.

Fat, in stew, soup, or gravy—too much

Drop in ice cubes; the grease will stick to them. Remove quickly.

Or: Wrap ice cubes in paper towels and draw over the surface. The fat will begin to solidify and stick to the paper towel. Repeat until enough fat is removed.

Or: Place paper towel lightly on surface and allow to absorb fat, then remove.

Or: Use a flat lettuce leaf the same way.

Or: Refrigerate dish. When cool, skim solidified fat from the top surface. Continue with recipe.

Garlic and onion

If you used too much garlic, simmer a sprig or small bunch of parsley in stew or soup for 10 minutes.

Or: To remove onion and garlic flavors from hands, pots, and pans, chopping boards, etc., rub with salt, lemon juice, or vinegar.

Or: To remove onion and garlic from hands, rub hands on stainless steel.

Ketchup, in a sauce—too much

Add lemon juice to mask the ketchup taste. You may also add a bit of sugar to counteract the acidity of the lemon.

Potatoes turn brown after slicing

Cook them in milk to whiten.

Radishes have become soft

Cover with water and place in refrigerator.

Rice looks dingy and not white

Add lemon juice to cooking water.

Salty dish

Add a peeled, thinly sliced potato to the salty dish and boil until the potato appears transparent. Remove the potato slices.

Or: If fish is too salty, add vinegar to the cooking liquid.

Or: For a tomato dish, add more peeled tomatoes to absorb the salt. Leave in dish if appropriate.

Or: For items like soup, stew, or tomato sauce, add pinches of brown sugar to taste.

Sugar has become dried and hard

Dampen a paper towel and place with sugar in a sealed plastic bag until sugar is soft.

Tomato—too much

Add lemon juice to mask some of the tomato taste. Add a bit of sugar to cut the lemon's acidity.

Too spicy

In the pot, add salt. On the tongue, lips, or mouth, a little sugar, buttermilk, milk, bread, or crackers will help neutralize the spiciness.

Vegetables are in danger of being overcooked

Drain and run very cold water over them immediately.

Whipped cream separated

Fold in 1 tablespoon cream until texture improves.

Household Formulas

Do you really need another concoction of costly, bottled chemicals? You already have most of the ingredients for household cleansers and stain removers in your kitchen or cleaning cupboard. Many common household ingredients are great alternatives to commercial cleaning products. These ingredients are nontoxic, readily available, less expensive, and can be mixed up in any amount at a moment's notice.

Note: Check for hardiness and colorfastness of materials before using these formulas.

Air freshener
Bake orange peels at 350°F for 10 minutes.

Or: Place a sliced orange, grapefruit, or lemon in a pan of water and boil gently for an hour.

Or: Place bowls of baking soda or activated charcoal around the house.

Or: Pour vinegar into an uncovered dish.

Air freshener spray

In a spray bottle dissolve 1 teaspoon baking soda and 1 teaspoon lemon juice in 2 cups hot water (do not spray on fabrics).

All-purpose cleanser

$\frac{1}{2}$ cup Borax

1 gallon warm water

Or:

$\frac{1}{2}$ cup ammonia

$\frac{1}{4}$ cup vinegar

2 tablespoons baking soda

1 gallon warm water

Note: Good for floors.

Or:

$\frac{1}{2}$ cup ammonia

$\frac{1}{2}$ cup washing soda

1 gallon warm water

Bathroom cleanser

Dip damp sponge in baking soda.

Black lacquer cleanser

Dip a cloth in a strong tea solution and rub well.

Bottle cleaner

To clean out the inside of a bottle, put in 2 tablespoons kosher or other coarse salt and $\frac{1}{4}$ cup lukewarm water, cap bottle, and shake vigorously. When salt starts to dissolve, pour out, and rinse bottle. Repeat as necessary.

Brass cleanser
Rub hard with lemon juice and salt.

Or: Spread with ketchup, let stand 10 minutes, and then rub hard.

Breadbox cleanser
2 tablespoons vinegar in 1 quart water.

Note: This also deters mold.

Carpet deodorizer
1 cup baking soda or 1 cup cornstarch

Sprinkle on carpet. Wait 30 minutes and vacuum.

Chrome cleanser
Make a paste of baking soda and water.

Or: Use the fresh-squeezed rind of a lemon.

Or: Use vinegar.

Copper cleanser
Spread with a paste of lemon juice or vinegar, salt, and flour, or spread with ketchup. Let stand 10 minutes and rub hard.

Crystal cleanser
Use a mixture of half rubbing alcohol, half water. Do not rinse.

Cutting boards

Rub with baking soda. Spray with vinegar, let sit 5 minutes, and rinse with water.

Deodorant

After bathing, sprinkle some baking soda in your hands and rub under your arms.

Disinfectant

Use $\frac{1}{2}$ cup Borax in 1 gallon hot water.

Or: use 1 cup laundry bleach in 1 gallon hot water.

Drain cleaner

$\frac{1}{2}$ cup salt

$\frac{1}{2}$ cup vinegar

Pour down drain, followed by 2 quarts boiling water.

Drain freshener

Pour $\frac{1}{2}$ cup baking soda down the drain. After 2 minutes pour in $\frac{1}{2}$ cup vinegar followed by 2 quarts of boiling water.

Drain opener

Dump 1 cup baking soda down drain, followed by 1 cup vinegar. Cover drain lightly. When fizzing stops, pour boiling water down drain.

Dusting cloth

Lightly moisten cloth and rub. For very soiled items such as woodwork or furniture, use a mixture of equal parts olive oil and vinegar sprinkled lightly on a cloth.

Fertilizer

1 tablespoon Epsom salts
1 tablespoon baking soda
1 ½ teaspoons household ammonia
3 gallons water

Floor cleaner

½ cup vinegar
½ gallon warm water
Or:
¼ cup washing soda
½ tablespoon liquid soap
¼ cup vinegar
2 gallons hot water

Floor shiner

½ cup cornstarch
1 gallon lukewarm water

Furniture cleaner for natural wood

1 cup cooled strong black tea
¼ cup vinegar

Furniture polish

⅔ cup olive oil or mineral or linseed oil or walnut oil

⅓ cup lemon juice or 1 teaspoon lemon oil
Rub in well, then rub off residue with a clean cloth.

Glass cleaner
See Window cleanser

Hard water deposit remover
Soak item in white vinegar or a half-and-half solution of white vinegar and water.

Iron (electric) stain remover (not for nonstick coatings)
On a cold iron, use equal parts vinegar and salt on a cloth, or use baking soda on a nonabrasive scouring pad.

Mildew remover
½ cup vinegar and ½ cup Borax in warm water
 Or: ½ cup laundry bleach in ½ gallon warm water

Mouth freshener
Chew on a sprig of parsley, or on whole cloves or fennel seeds.

Mouthwash
Gargle with equal parts hydrogen peroxide and water.
 Note: Do not swallow.

Nonstick pan cleanser
Use baking soda on a nonabrasive scouring pad.

Oven cleaner, for non-self-cleaning ovens

Pour ½ cup ammonia into a bowl. Set in cold oven overnight. Next morning, mix the ammonia with 1 quart warm water and wipe off inside of oven. Do this in well-ventilated area.

Or: Mix equal parts baking soda and salt. Scrub with a damp sponge.

Pesticide/deterrent for cockroaches, silverfish, or earwigs

Dust cracks and crevices with a fine layer of boric acid or diatomaceous earth.

Note: Keep out of reach of children.

Or: Combine equal parts sugar and baking soda and set out as a trap for insects.

Note: Keep out of reach of children.

Pesticide for ants

1 teaspoon liquid soap

1 quart water

Mix in a spray bottle.

Use Vaseline or dish soap to block up entry holes.

Pewter polish

Mix equal parts salt and flour and make a paste using vinegar. Rub on, let dry, rinse in hot water.

Or: Take dampened cabbage leaves, sprinkle them with salt, and rub on the pewter.

Pot and pan cleanser

Soak in white vinegar for 30 minutes.

Refrigerator and freezer deodorizer

Place opened container of baking soda in refrigerator or freezer. Replace after 3 months.

Or: Place dampened, crumpled newspapers in refrigerator. Replace every 24 hours until smell is gone.

Or: Place slices of white bread in the refrigerator. Replace periodically until smell is gone.

Refrigerator cleanser

1 tablespoon Borax
1 quart water
Or:
1 tablespoon baking soda
1 quart water

Scouring powder

Use baking soda.
Or:
1 cup baking soda
1 cup salt
Mix together. Store in an airtight container.

Silver cleanser

Make paste of baking soda and water. Apply with damp sponge or cloth and continue rubbing until clean.

Or: Use toothpaste and a soft-bristled toothbrush.

Silver polish
Place silver in a pan and cover with water. Add 2 tablespoons salt, 2 tablespoons baking soda, and a few sheets of aluminum foil. Let stand for an hour or more until tarnish disappears.

Or: Add a few drops of vegetable oil to a small amount of toothpaste and polish with a soft toothbrush.

Or: For silver jewelry, soak in lemon juice or vinegar. Rinse with warm water and dry immediately.

Soft scrub
Make a paste from $1/2$ cup baking soda and liquid soap.

Spot remover
$1/2$ cup Borax mixed with 2 cups cold water

Spray cleaner, grease cutting
1 quart hot water
2 teaspoons Borax
1 teaspoon washing soda
$1/4$ cup vinegar
1 teaspoon liquid soap
Combine in a spray bottle.

Spray cleaner, strong
1 quart hot water
1 tablespoon Borax
$3/8$ cup vinegar
Combine in a spray bottle.

Stainless steel cleanser

Use ammonia and hot water, mixed with a mild, non-chlorinated, nonabrasive cleanser.

Or: To remove spots, rub with a cloth dampened with white vinegar.

Stain remover, blood

Rub under cold, running water with mild soap.

Rub with hydrogen peroxide.

Note: This may bleach certain items.

Or: Soak with $\frac{1}{2}$ cup Borax dissolved in 2 cups cold water.

Or: Make a paste of cornstarch or talcum powder and water. Let dry on stain and brush off.

Or: Sprinkle with meat tenderizer and water. Sponge off after 30 minutes.

Stain remover, chocolate

Use hot, soapy water.

Or: Use hydrogen peroxide.

Note: This may bleach fabric.

Stain remover, coffee

Rub fabric with cloth saturated with beaten egg yolk or denatured alcohol. Rinse with water.

Or: Make a paste of Borax and hot water and rub into the stain.

Or: Dampen with club soda and sprinkle with salt.

Stain remover, fruit and wine

Dampen with club soda.

Stain remover, grass

Soak in vinegar.

Stain remover, grease

Sprinkle fabric with cornstarch or talcum powder. After 2 hours, brush off.

Or: Dampen with club soda and rub lightly. Rinse. Repeat if necessary.

Stain remover, ink

Soak in milk.

Or: Soak in lemon juice.

Stain remover, perspiration

Make a paste of salt and water and rub on stain.

Or: Make a paste of baking soda and salt and rub on stain.

Or: Use vinegar.

Stain remover, tea

Pour very hot water on fabric from a height of at least 3 feet.

Stain remover, wine

Pour club soda on stain, then rinse.

Toilet bowl cleanser

Use 4 tablespoons baking soda plus 1 cup vinegar.

Or: Use 1 cup Borax. Let sit overnight.

Toothpaste

Make a paste of baking soda and water.

Or: Make a paste of baking soda, salt, and water.

Tub and tile cleanser

Rub with half a lemon dipped in Borax.

Varnished woodwork and furniture

Tea, steeped 30 to 40 minutes. Rub on with cloth.

Water spots on dishes

Add vinegar to rinse water.

Water stains on furniture

Rub with toothpaste.

Window cleanser

Mix $1/2$ cup white or cider vinegar in $1/2$ gallon water. Spray on windows and wipe with crumpled newspaper.

Or: Use 1 tablespoon ammonia in 2 cups water. Wear protective gloves while you clean.

Woodwork cleanser

1 teaspoon white vinegar in 1 quart water

About the Author

Cicely Hall

As a food lover, Becky Sue Epstein is always ready to explore new recipes and create new dishes, which is why she started collecting the kitchen substitutions that eventually turned into the book *Substituting Ingredients*.

As a writer, she contributes articles on food, travel, wine, and spirits to publications in various parts of the world; she began her career as a restaurant reviewer in Los Angeles while working in film and television there.

Currently, Epstein is an editor for several national magazines and online publications. In between trips and tastings, she writes books in her hometown of Lexington, Massachusetts. Her most recent cookbook is *The American Lighthouse Cookbook* (Sourcebooks/Cumberland House), and she is currently working on a history of champagne and sparkling wine. Visit her website at www.BeckySueEpstein.com.